W9-CKH-409

DATE DUE

Rf
D

DOSTOEVSKY
AND THE
CATHOLIC
CHURCH

DENIS DIRSCHERL, S.J.

Loyola University Press
Chicago

© Denis Dirscherl
All rights reserved
Printed in the United States of America

Loyola University Press
3441 North Ashland Avenue
Chicago, Illinois 60657

Library of Congress Cataloging-in-Publication Data
Dirscherl, Denis.
  Dostoevsky and the Catholic Church.
  Includes index.
  Bibliography: p. 157
  1. Dostoyevsky, Fuyodor, 1821-1881—Religion.
2. Anti-Catholicism in literature. 3. Dostoevsky, Fyodor,
1821-1881—Biography. 4. Novelists, Russian—19th
century—Biography. I. Title.
PG3328.Z7R4226   1986   891.73'3   86-2961
ISBN 0-8294-0502-X

TO MY MOTHER,
MARGARET

CONTENTS

Two
Dostoevsky: Prophet of Russian Orthodoxy

Three
Dostoevsky and the Catholic Pax Romana

PREFACE

The multifaceted ideas of Dostoevsky have been on my mind since my early military days. They pursued me through college and seminary years, and into a later career in the military with the United States Air Force. Although the problems and the ideas involved in this book are delicate, for they touch on the deepest faith and religious concerns of many men and women, the research, reflection, and writing of this project was a very happy experience. The original draft proved to be a fitting climax to my doctoral studies at Georgetown University; the freedom and flexibility of the then chairman of the Russian Area Studies Program, the late Professor Joseph Schiebel, my two readers, Professor Frank Fadner and Professor Sergei Livitsky, and most especially my mentor and advisor, Professor, and Russian Orthodox priest, Dmitri Grigorieff made this possible. For allowing me the utmost freedom in my own interpretation, I hold all four professors in the highest esteem.

INTRODUCTION

No Russian writer has so poignantly expressed his country's ambiguous and often painful relationship with the West as Fyodor Dostoevsky. Indeed, few writers of his era so deliberately wrestled with the "Western problem." His critique, his final resolution on the Europe of his day, as is commonly known, focused on what he believed was the ultimate source of this alien spirit: the Roman Catholic Church.

Dostoevsky used his creative genius and "cruel talent" to portray the spirit that he believed characterized the mass of humanity beyond the borders of Russia. Those who reside in the West, those who proclaim allegiance to Western ideals may not understand or accept his devastating attack, one could say literary vivisection. Yet many issues which Dostoevsky raised are the large questions which still face us in the second half of the twentieth century. His questions are timeless.

Especially in the late sixties and early seventies, with his publication of *The Idiot* and *The Possessed*, Dostoevsky aimed his thrust at the use of power and force by the Catholic Church, both in her centuries-old development and in the pragmatic policies of the Church of his day. The image projected suggested for Dostoevsky an imminent apocalypse—a showdown of ideologies, perhaps even a breakdown of historical forces.

Dostoevsky saw the Catholic Church through the eyes of a long-standing Russian tradition in an atmosphere polluted by ten centuries of polemics. This problematic is the point of departure and the first chapter of our study: to properly understand Dostoevsky's convictions about the spirit of the West, one must deal with the historical animosity that developed and spread in the Russian consciousness since the birth of Christianity in the vast land once called Rus'. The first task is to locate and recount the sources of the animosity and hostility toward the Catholic Church that so strongly influenced the Russians' worldview up to Dostoevsky's day.

But Dostoevsky looked to the East as well as to the West. Religious issues were always close to his heart, especially in the second half of his life. Dostoevsky time and time again expressed his high esteem for and firm adherence to the spirit of Orthodoxy; only from it could salvation come to him and his people. Gradually he developed his own peculiar conception of the Orthodox Church—of its chief characteristics, its historical trends, and its distinctive role in the modern world. Dostoevsky believed in "Holy Russia." He believed that his native Russia would offer the "word" of reconciliation for all mankind, and he evolved one of the most attractive religious élans of any religion. The development of these ideas in relation to his personal life and faith inform the second chapter.

The third chapter proceeds both by logical analysis and chronological reconstruction of Dostoevsky's view of the Christian West. The preliminary steps are quite personal since Dostoevsky spent some crucial years in Europe. It describes his general critique of the West, and then shifts its focus to Dostoevsky's fierce, combative attack on the Catholic Church's alleged lust for power. Here, the chief attributes of the papacy and the Jesuits, both props and symbols of Roman power, come under careful scrutiny. The work closes with a brief critique of Dostoevsky's own views.

The reader will note that some citations have dates for both the Julian and Gregorian calendars. Such citations are found in the sources, generally writings aimed at both a Russian and a European audience. The Soviet Union adopted the Gregorian calendar in 1918; consequently, most Russian nineteenth-century sources follow the Julian calendar.

The system of notes is twofold. To make this book easier to use, references to literary works are in the text; references to monographs and background material are in the endnotes. Where no credit is given, the translation is that of the author.

The corpus of Dostoevsky—articles, letters, and books—and the commentary it has inspired are vast. But until now, there has been no straightforward attempt to understand the significant aspects of ecclesiastical and religious conflict with the West in general and the Catholic Church in particular, as reflected in Dostoevsky. For the most part, only fragmentary articles farced with striking statements by Dostoevsky have been presented. Here the task is not only to re-count the religious conflict as seen by Dostoevsky, but also to indicate its historical underpinnings. Within this background it was quite natural, almost inevitable, for Dostoevsky to write and say what he did.

As the literary world has already observed many anniversaries of this prolific and powerful writer, I hope that this study, with the combined disciplines of Russian history, literature, philosophy, and theology will more adequately reveal the essential word of Dostoevsky on the Christian West. For his views underlie many problems that separate East and West in our epoch, however deep in the subconscious level they may lie.

ONE

A POLEMICAL TRADITION

Introduction

One of the most celebrated annals of Russian history is the Kievan *Povest' vremennykh let—The Tale of Bygone Years*, or *The Primary Chronicle*.[1] It roots Christian Russia in the legendary ministry of Andrew the Apostle.

> When Andrew was teaching in Sinope and came to Kherson (as has been recounted elsewhere), he observed that the mouth of the Dnieper was near by. Conceiving a desire to go to Rome, he thus journeyed to the mouth of the Dnieper. Thence he ascended the river, and by chance he halted beneath the hills upon the shore. Upon arising in the morning, he observed to the disciples who were with him, "See ye these hills? So shall the favor of God shine upon them that on this spot a great city [Kiev] shall arise, and God shall erect many churches therein."[2]

Kiev did indeed rise in splendor under the "Russian Charlemagne," Vladimir, but its roots are not as simple as the *Chronicle* would have it.

The twelfth century *Chronicle* exemplifies the preoccupation of Latins and Greeks with finding heresy in each other's teaching and polemics, and their often openly one-sided re-creation of historical events. To match Rome's claim of primacy in the Church, and Antioch, Alexandria, and Jerusalem in the East, the Byzantines used a counter tradition that one of the original twelve apostles, St. Andrew, brought Christianity to the East. Andrew was the first apostle to whom the Lord had addressed his invitation to become his disciple (John 1:37–42), and Andrew introduced his brother Simon Peter to Christ; the Byzantines therefore considered their episcopal see as equal, if not superior, to that of Rome.[3]

Historians today believe that the *Chronicle* was composed by various authors; Nestor (c. 1056–Oct. 27, 1113), a monk of the Monastery of the Caves in Kiev, was one of the most prominent. The author of the *Chronicle* was a militant churchman who believed that Byzantine Orthodoxy was the only pure source of enlightenment for the entire world. He was no dispassionate scholar but an experienced controversialist who wrote a biased story of Russia's conversion with the avowed intention of influencing the future of his country. Yet he disguised his prejudices as impartial and well-documented history.[4]

This background chapter shows the polemical and inimical tradition that developed and expanded in the Russian consciousness from the very beginnings. Their causes, justifications, motives, and rationalizations necessarily assume secondary importance as we trace the outlines of Russian church history through its Varangian origin, the Byzantine hegemony, and the Mongol and post-Mongol periods.

The Varangian Origins of Kievan Rus'

Christianity came to Rus' at least by the middle of the ninth century. Possibly early Christianity in ancient Rus' was of the Cyrilo-Methodian rite.[5] A bishopric was established at Kiev for Norsemen and Slavs when Askold and Dir and other leaders became Christians.[6] The new creed did not remain long, however, as northern pagan influence wiped out the new religion and had to wait another century before starting anew.

Olga, Vladimir's grandmother, was the first of the Kiev ruling house to be converted; she preserved the life of Christianity in Kievan Russia. According to *The Primary Chronicle*, 82, Olga was baptized in Constantinople—around 957, Dvornik believes.[7] Others opt for the Slavonic rite.[8] According to Jugie, St. Olga may have shared the Latin rite with the early Varangian Christians.[9] She asked Otto I of Germany for priests and a bishop, but the mission failed through delay and pagan opposition. Kartashev denies Jugie's speculation;[10] indeed, most native Russian writers tend to deny or minimize Latin or Roman influence in early Rus' Church history.[11]

Her son Svyatoslav had no time for the new religion: he preferred military exploits and feared the mockery of his fellow warriors. Again, the mere acceptance of Christianity by Vladimir for the entirety of ancient Rus' around 988 was encased in an aura of semipolemical literature. "In general terms, the source evidence for the history of the Russian church from 988 to 1037 is both scarce and confused. No less contradictory is the information concerning the time and place of Vladimir's baptism."[12] According to the *Chronicle*, "Vladimir was baptized in the Church of St. Basil, which stands at Kherson upon a square in the center of the city, where the Khersonians trade."[13]

In any event, Vladimir accepted Christianity in exchange for the hand of Anna Porphyrogenita, sister of Emperor Basil. "Of course Basil did not give his sister in marriage to a northern barbarian and pagan merely because he desired to see Vladimir and his country christianized. The Byzantine *basileus* was not only a missionary, but first of all a statesman; therefore some change in relations between Byzantium and Russia must have taken place, and a change not in favor of the young northern state."[14]

In the apocryphal account of the conversion of Vladimir, the prince dispatched agents to find the true faith. They said:

> [we] went among the Germans, and saw them performing many ceremonies in their temples; but we beheld no glory there. Then we went to Greece, and the Greeks led us to the edifices where they worship their God, and we knew not whether we were in heaven or on earth. For on earth there is no such splendor or such beauty, and we are at a loss how to describe it. We only know that God dwells there among men, and their service is fairer than ceremonies of other nations. For we cannot forget that beauty.[15]

The legendary account of Vladimir choosing Christianity for ancient Rus' contains a dialogue between the prince and German emissaries:

Then came the Germans, asserting that they were come as emissaries of the Pope. They added, "Thus says the Pope: "Your country is like our country, but your faith is not as ours. For our faith is the light. We worship God, who has made heaven and earth, the stars, the moon, and every creature, while your gods are only wood." Vladimir inquired what their teaching was. They replied, "fasting according to one's strength. But whatever one eats or drinks is all to the glory of God, as our teacher Paul has said." Then Vladimir answered, "Depart hence; our fathers accepted no such principle."[16]

The *Chronicle* also pictures Greek scholars instructing Vladimir on the true aspects of Christianity, pointing out that the Latins "commune with wafers, called *oplatki* which God did not give them, for he ordained that we should commune with bread." Vladimir is exhorted to "avoid the deceit of heretics" and instructed not to

accept the teachings of the Latins, whose instruction is vicious. For when they enter the church, they do not kneel before the images, but they stand upright before kneeling, and when they have knelt, they trace a cross on the ground and then kiss it, but they stand on it when they arise. Thus while prostrate they kiss it, and yet upon arising they trample it underfoot. Such is not the tradition of the Apostles. For the Apostles prescribed the kissing of an upright cross, and also prescribed the use of images. For the Evangelist Luke painted the first image and sent it to Rome. As Basil has said, the honor rendered to the image redounds to its original.[17]

The controversial atmosphere of the accounts in the *Chronicle* indicates the ideas that filtered into ancient Rus' from Byzantium. It is anachronistic to picture eastern and western Christianity before 1054 as distinct or different. Vladimir had several options of which rite he wished to observe and consequently which jurisdiction he wished to serve under.[18] Under Vladimir, Rus' entertained normal relations with the West and the papacy. At least four apal envoys visited Rus' (980–1001) during the early part of Vladimir's reign.[19]

In pre-Mongol Rus' the East Slavs did not immediately follow the lead of the Byzantines and consequently expressed little hostility toward the West and the Latin Church. Rather, Kiev remained a center of commerce where East and West crossed their trade routes. Yaroslav's daughter married the first Catholic King of Sweden; his other daughters became the wives of the kings of France, Hungary, and Norway while his sons married into German, Polish, and other European lines. Between the tenth and midthirteenth centuries, the Rurik line married into a host of foreign lines, thirty-four Polish spouses, fifteen Hungarian, thirteen German, thirteen Scandinavian and English, twelve Byzantine, and six Czech.[20]

By the tenth and eleventh centuries, translations of Latin and Slavonic works made their way into Kievan Rus'; for instance, the *Life of St. Wenceslas* and the *Life of St. Vitus*. Wenceslas and Ludmila, two Czech saints, were especially popular in eleventh century Rus'.[21] After Izyaslav (1054–78), Yaroslav's eldest son, lost power in Kiev on two occasions, he sent his son to appeal for aid from Pope Gregory VII in ᵗhe late 1070s.

Byzantine Ecclesiastical Dominance

The eventual Greek dominance over the Rus' Church begins in the late eleventh century when Rus' anti-Latin literature begins to appear. Under the influence of the Greek metropolitans, everything associated with Rome is depicted in black colors. The Latins are hostile opponents. Gradually the East Slavs begin to acquire a distaste for Catholics of the West.[22]

Subtle means sometimes concealed the animosity—for instance, the glossing over of early Roman Catholic influence in East Slavic lands, or the distorting of the values and activities of certain saints, by suggesting that the Czech St. Adalbert, popular in eleventh century Rus', was responsible for suppressing the Slavonic liturgy.[23]

Kievan Metropolitan George (1070–80) banned marriages between Russian Orthodox and Roman Catholics, declaring that "old Rome" fell into heresy under German domination. He drew up a list of twenty-seven different errors, and sent it both to his confreres and to Rome. The metropolitan of Kiev, Nicephorus (1104–21), submitted twenty reasons in explaining the heresy of the Latins and advised his secular counterpart, Vladimir Monomakh, to read his treatise, "not once, but twice, and even more."[24] The same Nicephorus advised Yaroslav, the prince of Volynia, to beware of sinful contacts with the Latins who had abandoned the apostolic Church.

Writing to Prince Izyaslav of Kiev, Theodosius of Pechersk

(d. 1074) declared that "the Latins have polluted the whole world." Another writer intimated that the devil takes the form of a Pole when he wishes to tempt the Russian ascetics. Further north, the Pskov chronicles referred to Catholics as those "pagan Latins," or the "pagan Germans," or "godless Germans." Indeed, the Pskovians expelled one of their princes for allowing his daughter to marry a Catholic.[25]

Probably the most creative and effective of the early controversial literature came from the pen of the Abbot Daniel in *Pilgrimage to Palestine*. His description includes a telling incident of how a "light from heaven" descended on the tomb of Christ during Holy Saturday ceremonies. Daniel declares that this heavenly light ignited both the Greek lamps and the lamp that Daniel himself placed there for Kievan Rus. But the Frankish lamps, representing the Latins, were not lighted; divine grace and blessings had been denied to the West.[26] Daniel made the journey between 1106 and 1108. This peculiar typology was destined to grow and develop in the coming centuries and came to full blossom in early sixteenth and seventeenth century Muscovy.

Among the early charges brought against the Latins was their shaving off beards, having more than one altar in churches, breaking fasting regulations, and bishops and priests shedding blood in battle. Lengthy lists were compiled to substantiate the charges of apostasy against the Roman Church.[27] In brief, the Greek missionaries advised the early inhabitants of Rus' to eschew contact with Latin Catholics, not to kiss them, not to fraternize with them, not to defer to them, and not to eat out of the same dish with them.[28]

The deepening estrangement of Eastern and Western Christianity before and after the confrontation between Patriarch Michael Caerularius and Cardinal Humbert in 1054 have enormous significance for the birth and development of Christianity in Russia. In the wake of strained relations and mutual misunderstandings, Russia became the spiritual heir of Byzantium and thereby acquired a ready-made polemical tradition.[29] For Byzantium, the West fell under the domination of the barbarians and Rome itself was captured; barbarian Rome was no longer considered a part of the empire, and no longer an expression of the Roman idea, which survived only in Constantinople.[30] By refusing to accept each other, Constantinople and Rome broke down the essential psychological atmosphere for enduring communication. Contemporary historians view the rift between Rome and Byzantium in 1054 as symptomatic of longstanding problems which intensified thereafter.[31]

According to the Greeks, the Latin faith was no better than Judaism [Zhidovstva] and consequently there was no salvation in Rome. No one contested the instruction of the Greeks because no one was competent to counter an opinion seemingly shared by the whole Greek Church.[31] All the anti-Catholic polemics circulated then in Kievan Rus' were either translated from Greek or written by Greeks in Russia.[33]

The Growth in Division

The pattern of Kievan Rus' and the East Slavs changed drasticly in the thirteenth century. The fourth Crusade in 1204 intensified and crystallized the religious rift. For the Orthodox, the Latins were nothing more than barbarians and savages for perpetrating the horrible spectacle in Constantinople.[34] "The schism did not become truly definitive, it would seem, until as late as 1204, when the Latins captured Constantinople and forced the Greek population to accept Roman Catholicism. On the lower levels in fact, the ordinary man of East and West was hardly even aware of any religious rupture until long after 1054 and probably not until well into the twelfth century."[35]

From the West came other armies and crusades, notably the military orders of the Brothers of the Sword who merged in 1237 with the Teutonic Knights. Both moved into Livonia and Lithuania fighting for faith and dominion as they enforced Christianity on the pagans. Though these new warriors posed a serious threat for only brief spells, their combined pressure in the Baltic and northern fringe of Rus' with the Mongol movement in the South created a traumatic experience for the rulers and inhabitants of Rus'.[36]

The Knights believed that the Orthodox needed salvation as much as the pagans.[37] When Saint Alexander Nevsky routed the Swedes in 1240 and the Teutonic Knights two years later, this great warrior and later patron of St. Petersburg naturally became a hero of both church and people. The *Life of Alexander*, which focused on the military prowess of their leader in defense of Orthodoxy, quite readily assumed an anti-Catholic posture fostered by the battle.[38]

The Mongolian Dominance

While the Knights continued to harass the northwestern borders of Rus', the Mongol invasion in the south brought more havoc and quickened the twilight of Kievan Rus'. "The Mongol conquest is the most fateful catastrophe suffered by Russia during her entire history. The whole character of her life—social, political, and cultural—changed during this period. Even the geographical focus of Russian history shifted from Kiev to the northeast."[39] The ideology of the Mongol Horde deserves special mention. The Mongols built their empire not to engage in power-politics, or to secure military and economic domination over the world, but to carry out the will of God. The Mongol khans did not enter into the relation of one sovereign ruler to another, but into the relation of a messenger of God to the ignorant.[40]

Though the Mongols effectively controled Rus' for several centuries, the bulk of the horde remained in Asia. Their ratio was about one to a hundred.[41] The Mongols gave the Rus' Church a privileged place in East Slav society.

> In exchange for prayers the Khans of the Golden Horde bestowed large economic and social privileges upon the Russian Church: they exempted the clergy as a whole from paying taxes; they gave the bishops extensive jurisdiction over all the population dependent on the Church. Never before or after the Mongol domination, did the Russian Church enjoy such privileges, and the metropolitans of Moscow carefully preserved in their archives the so-called *Yarlyks*—the charters of the Khans.[42]

Most important, the Mongol period helped simpify East Slav and Rus' ambivalence toward Rome. Byzantine ideas and influence continued as before. Greek metropolitans provided church leadership, and native candidates journeyed to Byzantium seeking the blessing and advice of the patriarch residing there. Under these circumstances Russian political dependence upon Byzantium disappeared; yet still the metropolitan was sent to Russia from Constantinople, and became the sole representative of the empire and of the idea of the universal power of the emperor.[43]

The Mongols suffered a brief setback in 1380 at the hands of Dmitri Donskoy, but they quickly recovered and maintained their power for the rest of the fourteenth century. When factions and internecine warfare weakened their power in the fifteenth century, Muscovy filled the power vacuum by centralizing and superseding the rival principalities of Novgorod, Rostov, Suzdal and Tver.

Attempts at Reconciliation

Though Rome and Byzantium attempted brief reunions after the fourth Crusade in 1204 and again at the Second Council of Lyons in 1274, Rome and the new center of power in Moscow were chasms apart. As the secular center of influence moved north, from Kiev, to Vladimir, the ecclesiastical hierarchy followed suit. Metropolitan Peter was buried there in 1326, and Moscow became the ecclesiastical capital, although the metropolitan's title remained "of Kiev and all Russia." Ivan I Kalita added "and of all Russia" to his title of grand duke of Muskovy, a symbol of a drive for hegemony by Moscow.[44]

The new object of anxious attention during the Mongol occupation was the religious question in the borderlands of eastern Europe: Galicia, Lithuania, and Poland. In 1324 Pope John XXII made fresh attempts to reunite eastern Europe to Rome. Kiev was restored by the non-Christian Lithuanian Prince Gedimin (1316–41) and Galicia merged with the Polish kingdom under Casimir III (1333–70). When Jagello married Queen Hedwig of Poland in 1386 and joined the Latin camp, prospects of reunion grew apace. Under the new title of Vladislav II, Jagello ruled over a Catholic Poland and Lithuania until 1434.

As Latin pressure for reunion was more steadily applied in the West and North during the fourteenth century, hostilities between Rome and Rus' continued to be the norm. In 1347, for instance, the Swedish King Magnus attempted to expand the Latin faith in the Novgorod area. Sailing in with his troops, he announced to the inhabitants of Novgorod: "Send your philosophers to a conference, and I will send our own; let them judge about the faith; I want to know what faith is better. If it seems that your faith is better I will accept yours; but if ours is better, you will accept ours,—and we will all be as one man. But if you do not accept our faith, then I will set upon you with all our might."[45]

The burgeoning secular and ecclesiastical power of the Poland-Lithuania Union under Vladislav II soon provoked further dissension and rivalry between Latins and Orthodox. Catholicism became the official state religion in Lithuania whereby political privileges were restricted to Catholics.[46] Pressure was soon exerted to divide the Russian metropolitanate. Naturally this division tended to encourage reunion between Rome and the Orthodox living outside Rus' proper. These attempts to split the orthodox had an earlier tradition, notably in the Galician and Volynian areas while Andronik Paleolog ruled Constantinople from 1282 to 1327. Under Patriarch Ioann Glik (1316–20), another metropolitanate was opened in Lithuania. And the Lithuanian Prince Olgerd (1341–80), successor to Gedimin, received approval to establish a relative of his wife, Roman, as metropolitan over a vast area of his domain.[47] Among the reasons for Russians leaving Lithuania for Moscow, religion did not play a prominent part. A secondary reason which may have helped to produce the decision of the West Russian nobles to desert Lithuania for Moscow was the preferred position of Catholicism, but it rarely played a decisive role. Although considerable anti-Orthodox prejudice was evident in the period up through 1430, resentment against the Catholic Church does not seem to have been the primary motive for desertion.[48]

Alexis became metropolitan of Rus' in 1353, but political and ecclesiastical pressure created such turmoil toward the end of his life that the patriarch of Constantinople attempted a peaceful settlement by sending Cyprian to become metropolitan of Kiev while Alexis was still alive. When Alexis died, in 1378, Cyprian continued in office until his death in 1406. Vitold, Grand Duke of Lithuania (1392–1430) and a cousin of Vladislav II, and his successor Svidrigello both agitated for separate metropolitanates. Vitold, in particular, sought to succeed Cyprian with Gregory Camblak, a nephew of Cyprian. But because the Muscovites were on better terms with the Greeks at the moment, Photius (1408–31) was established in the post.

The Muscovite princes incessantly maneuvered for power and independence from Byzantium while at this same time being influenced by the ideology of "Caesarism" of second Rome. Basil had the name of emperor taken from the list mentioned during the liturgy, and Patriarch Anthony wrote a persuasive letter to have it restored:

> Therefore, my son, it is not loyal to say that we have the Church without a Basileus, because it is impossible for Christians to have a Church with no Basileus. The Basileia and the Church have so much in common that they cannot be separated. Christians can only repudiate emperors who are heretics, fight the Church or introduce doctrines irreconcilable with the teaching of the Apostles and the Fathers. But the great and holy autocrator, by the grace of God, is an Orthodox and a believer, a champion of the Church, its protector

and avenger, so that it is impossible for bishops not to mention him in the liturgy. Of whom then do the Fathers, the councils, and the canons speak? Always and everywhere they speak loudly of the one legitimate Basileus, whose laws, edicts, and charters are in force all the world over and who alone, and nobody else, is everywhere mentioned in the liturgy by the Christians.[49]

In 1415, in spite of his earlier rejection, Vitold and Vladislav II proclaimed Gregory metropolitan of Lithuania and in 1418 sent him to the Council of Constance to discus reunion. Thus with the opening and closing of the metropolitanates, confusion reigned to such a point that when Gerasim returned from Constantinople in 1433, the question raised was whether he was metropolitan of all Russia or only Lithuania.[50]

With the deaths of Photius and Gerasim, the Muscovites hoped to have a native Russian in the office of metropolitan and accordingly chose Jonah. For their part the Greeks chose one of their own, Isidore, from the monastery of St. Demetrius. The Greek decision prevailed, and with the selection of Isidore events of momentous outcome followed in the next half century, events that had an enormous impact on the Russian consciousness.

The Council of Florence

After Basil II (1425–1462) gave his reluctant permission and with the stipulation that there should be no alterations in the faith, Isidore left Moscow for Florence with more than two hundred Russians including the bishop of Suzdal, Abraham, and a representative of the grand duke of Tver. After lengthy discussions the Greek, Russian, and various other Eastern Christians were officially reunited with the Catholic Church at Florence, being accepted by the emperor and the patriarch of Constantinople, and Isidore representing Muscovy.[51]

The Greeks in the Council of Florence did not consider the primacy of the pope as its chief theological problem with the other churches, but the question of the procession of the Holy Spirit. Given the choice of subject for the doctrinal debates, they chose to discuss in Ferrara the legitimacy of the addition of the *Filioque* to the Creed. In Florence, after the transfer of the Council, all the public sessions (March 1439) were about the doctrine of the procession.[52]

Authorities on the subject center on the causes of the ephemeral nature of the union. All agree that politics had too much to say in the union. Religious sincerity was too often lacking; if the objectives of the papacy remained generally constant, the enthusiasm of the emperors for union ebbed and flowed with their need for Western aid.[53] The commotion caused by the refusal of Patriarch Joseph to kiss the foot of the Pope indicates the superficiality of the council. Indeed, the union was not formally proclaimed in Constantinople until the eve of its capture by the Turks in 1453.[54]

Isidore returned to Moscow on March 19, 1441, preceded by a Latin cross as he entered Moscow Cathedral and accompanied by the monk Simeon in chains for his anti-union activities, both ill omens. Basil accepted the letters of Pope Eugenius, but after a solemn liturgy and reading of the agreement of the union, Isidore's announcement was greeted with silence. Four days later Isidore was arrested on the charge of heresy, "seduced by the Devil," as the chronicles expressed it.[55]

The rulers of Moscow already then, exercised autocratic power, even in ecclesiastical matters; they simply waited for Basil's decision. That decision was accepted without hesitation, a fact which in view of the exceptional importance of the matter greatly contributed to strengthen even more the authority of the grand duke.[56]

Isidore's task was probably impossible. Basil's rejection of Isidore and his mission was probably purely political. Part of his life-long endeavor was the hegemony of all the Russian States, and of his expansionist policy. Success in that would be possible only if Moscow was also the spiritual center of all Ruthenians, and so the first essential was that the metropolitan of Kiev and all Russia should be one of his own subjects and resident in his territory. Vitold and Svidrigello of Lithuania had both had the same idea and for a similar reason. While Basil enhanced the power and prestige of the grand dukes of Muscovy, he was asked to subordinate himself to the Pope and become allied with his old enemies, Poland, Lithuania, and the Teutonic Knights. But there is even more to the rejection than that.

About the time of Florence. . . . . there were also tensions between the Russians and the Greeks. In spite of their reverence for the version of the Greek faith embodied by Mark of Ephesus, the Russians grew impatient with the tutelage of the Byzantines, who to them were not quite trustworthy in their religious demeanor, while their own faith was the purest of all in the world. On the other side, that of the other Church, the Greeks resented a situation which amounted to practical autocephaly among the Northern Barbarians."[57]

Members of his own synod including Jonah, his old rival for the metropolitanate, and his traveling companion, Abraham, Bishop of Suzdal, were appointed to decide the issue.

The rejection of Isidore and Florence by Basil further estranged Rome and Moscow; consequently, Moscow was further isolated from the West. More importantly, rejection of Florence provided Basil II with a political and religious wedge. Even more than any church figure, Basil became the champion and protector of Orthodoxy. As the compiler of the *Stepennaia Kniga* (Book of Degrees) or czar's genealogy presents the reaction to Isidore's explanation of the reunion, "all were silent." Basil was the only one to stand up for Orthodoxy; "there was found only one [man] zealous for God and His true law."[58] Parallels are found in the anonymous writer's "Discourse Against the Latins." Basil is praised as "the tsar crowned by God" who "confirms the Holy Church unassailable by those who act like wolves, seeking to destroy the faith, the true piety which shines in the land of Russia."[59]

Simeon of Suzdal, companion and foe of Isidore's views at Florence, also builds Basil's image as protector of Orthodoxy in his "Tale of Isidore's Council": "Rejoice, Orthodox Prince Vasiliy, you have stifled the Latin heresy and would not let it grow among Orthodox Christians.... Rejoice Prince Vasiliy, for you are renowned in all the Western lands and in Rome itself; you have glorified the Orthodox faith and the whole land of Russia...."[60]

In a letter dated 1451/52, Basil, as ruler and protector of people and church, informed Emperor Constantine Palaeologus of the election of Jonah as metropolitan of all Russia. In the letter Basil reinforced his own image by refering to his "ancestor (praroditel') the most blessed saint and equal to the apostles, the grand prince Vladimir," and calls him the autocrat of all Russian lands.[61]

Isolation of the Russian Church

With the news of the fall of Constantinople in 1453, the self-esteem of the grand prince of Muscovy and the Russian Orthodox Church received further bolstering and a new mentality. Here was perfect justification for the superiority of Russian Orthodoxy to the Greeks and their second Rome. As Metropolitan Jonah declared, "Constantinople has fallen because it has deserted the true Orthodox faith. But in Russia the faith still lives, the Faith of the Seven Councils as Constantinople gave it to the Great Prince Vladimir. There exists only one true Church on earth, the Church of Russia."[62]

Constantinople thus was justly punished for apostasy from the true faith. With the fall of second Rome, Muscovy paradoxically became even more heavily influenced by Byzantium. For Muscovy was now the true heir of the old empire and the old church as well, as sole representative and propagator of the true faith.[63] A selection from *Discourse Selected from Sacred Writings in Latin* by an unknown indicates the self-esteem attributed to the land of Rus'.

> And now in the latter Times, God-enlightened land of Rus', it behooves you and your people to rejoice in the universal subsolar radiance of true Orthodoxy in faith, arrayed in the illumination of piety, having the cloak of God upon you—the radiant grace of God—your arms filled with flowers blooming in God's, sight—God's, temples, holy churches shining like stars in the sky, nay, gleaming like the rays of the sun, adorned in splendor and glorified with selections from sacred song—under the dominion of the God-chosen, God-beloved, God-respected and God-enlightened and God-sent man who governs you in the righteous way of God-appointed law, and the divinely wise student of sacred rules, blessed zealot for God and furtherer of the true Orthodoxy by his piety, petitioner to the Most High in true faith, the God-invested and greatly ruling, faithful and pious Great Prince Vasily Vasilyevich, God-crowned in Orthodoxy, Tsar of all Rus'.[64]

Jonah, the unsuccessful candidate twelve years earlier for Isidore's post as metropolitan of Russia, was installed in 1448. The rupture between East and West grew as another conflict developed between the eastern and western sectors of the Orthodox Church. On September 3, 1458, Pope Pius appointed Gregory, who had accompanied Isidore to Moscow and succeeded him as hegumen of the monastery of St. Demetrius in Constantinople, as metropolitan of Kiev. Consecrated by the uniate patriarch in exile, Gregory Mammas, on October 15, 1458, he left for his new see on January 17, 1459.[65]

Gregory proceeded to Poland where Casimir accepted him as metropolitan of Kiev and all Russia. A move was made even to place Gregory in charge of the see of Jonah, for the patriarch of Constantinople sent a message to Moscow and Novgorod urging that Gregory be recognized as metropolitan of all Russia. Jonah regrouped his forces, however, and at a synod convened in 1459 the Muscovites declared Jonah metropolitan of Kiev and all Russia, and proclaimed the Russian Church independent from Constantinople. From this time Russian metropolitans were elected by bishops and confirmed by the grand prince; the secular rulers maintained their prestige and power in the new autocephalous church.[66]

In 1462, Ivan III, "autocrat" and "gatherer of the land," began one of the longest ruling periods in Russian history,. Under his leadership the Muscovites emancipated themselves from Mongol rule and began to consolidate Moscow control over Rus' cities and towns. The Mongol occupation of Rus' had wrought vast differences between East and West.

> For two centuries Russia fell out of European history—a long stretch in the life of any nation. At the same time the Byzantine empire, as a result of the Latin conquests, sank to its dissolution, so that Russia could expect little from a quarter that was once her main cultural inspiration. When at last Russia emerged from obscurity she could scarcely recognize the West which had in the meantime made long strides toward cultural maturity and grown equally ignorant of the East. Russia did the best to make up for lost time, but the difference had struck too deep to be leveled out completely. To a certain extent Russia has ever since remained a stranger to the European family of nations. Her aloofness and idiosyncracies date from that period. Her only chance of evolving in harmony with the rest of Europe occurred in the eleventh century and the opportunity was lost at the expense of both.[67]

Though cut off from contact with much of Western Europe and now more powerful than second Rome, the Russians had meanwhile become more Orthodox than the Greeks and even more hostile to other forms of Christianity. The Roman Church meant to them hostile Poles, Bulgarians and Swedes along the western frontiers. Although the Fourth Crusade had no direct effect on them, they were indignant about it. The West had not preserved them from the Mongols; now they were rescuing themselves without its help, indeed in spite of its hostility.[68] Ivan indicated the security of his position by reinforcing Moscow's isolation and independence from Byzantium in 1470 by declaring the Greek Patriarch "deprived of any right over our Church."[69]

Attempt at Reunion

Rome again tried to close the chasm between the two churches, by proposing a dynastic marriage. Sophia Palaeologina, niece of the last Byzantine emperor and a Catholic of the Florentine tradition, married in 1466 only to become a widow shortly thereafter. Sophia was an attractive candidate on several counts. For one she might help re-union efforts between Rome and Moscow, and to the Muscovites she would serve as a human link with both the imperial and the ecclesiastical lines of second Rome. Cardinal Bessarion and Gian-Battista della Volpe, therefore, started negotiations with Ivan III, a widower himself since 1467. Though the goals seemed plausible, too many false hopes were raised in Rome by Volpe—called Ivan Friazin in Moscow—who was using both sides for his own personal advantage. By arrangement Sophia proceeded to Moscow in the company of the papal legate Anthony. But when the metropolitan of Moscow, Philip, learned who was leading the entourage with a Latin cross, he threatened to leave the city. To Ivan he related: "If he comes in one gate of your city of Moscow preceded by his cross, I, your spiritual father, will leave by another."[70]

Rome's dreams proved to be a mirage as Sophia chose to follow the Byzantine observance while Ivan assumed the double eagle coat of arms of the Byzantine emperors. Ivan thus thwarted the intrigues of Rome and, like Basil, continued as champion of Russian Orthodoxy. His secular role also enjoyed a heightened success; Metropolitan Zosimus praise him in 1492: "The Emperor Constantine built a new Rome, Tsargrad; but the sovereign and autocrat of all the Russias, Ivan Vasilievitch, the New Constantine, has laid the foundation for a new city of Constantine, Moscow."[71]

The "Tale of the White Cowl" well states the theme that the ecclesiastical and imperial center of gravity shifted from Rome to Constantinople, and thence to Moscow. Apparently written toward the end of the fifteenth century by Gennadius, Archbishop of Novgorod, and his co-worker Dimitry Gerasimov, the tale complements the rising self-esteem and growing strength of Russian Orthodox ideology. Revised a number of times—at first a compensatory piece suggesting the spiritual superiority of Novgorod after the city lost its political independence to Moscow—and finally declared apocryphal at the Moscow Synod of 1666–67, the account discloses how Pope Sylvester cured Emperor Constantine of an incurable ailment and in gratitude the emperor places a white cowl, or monk's headgear, on Sylvester's head as a symbol of spiritual primacy. Thereafter the cowl becomes a special object of veneration. Various individuals attempt to destroy it or keep it for their own possession but are punished; one dies, another is attacked with worms. Later the cowl is removed from Rome "because of their Latin heresies." All the future glory of Russia is revealed by Pope Sylvester in a vision to the patriarch of Constantinople, Philotheus: "I was ordered by God to reveal to you the great mystery which will come to pass in the predestined time." Then he relates the prophetic message of old:

> The ancient city of Rome will break away from the Glory and faith of Christ because of its pride and ambition. In the new Rome, which will be the City of Constantinople, the Christian faith will also perish through the violence of the sons of Hagar. In the third Rome, which will be the land of Russia, the Grace of the Holy Spirit will be revealed. Know then, Philotheus, that all Christians will finally unite into one Russian nation because of its orthodoxy. Since ancient times and by the will of Constantine, Emperor of the Earth, the imperial crown of the imperial city is predestined to be given to the Russian tsar. And the Russian tsar will be elevated by God above other nations, and under his sway will be many heathen kings.[72]

Other literature of this period, such as the *Tales of the Babylonian Empire* and the *Legend of the Princes of Vladimir* emphasize the temporal hegemony of Muscovy. The former attempts to support the Byzantine and then Muscovite heirship to the universal world empire. Imperial rule and rank stemmed all the way back to Babylon with a Russian taking part in discovering the insignia. The *Legend of the Princes of Vladimir* enhances the same idea by tracing the Russian ruling genealogy not only back to Rurik but to Prus, an invented brother of Emperor Augustus.

Ironically, the monk Philotheus of the Eleazar Monastery in

Pskov became one of the most avid proponents of Muscovite supremacy, ironical because Moscow took away the independence of Pskov
by force of arms under Ivan III. Philotheus's famous formulation, fostered by the events and oratory during the demise of Constantinople
and the rise of Muscovy, exults in the glory of the third and last Rome.
Rus' had all along been subordinated to the spirit of the south, Byzantium. Then she was humiliated by the Mongols. Now all would see
her in her true honor, in her predestined place in the world:

> The Church of Old Rome fell because of the Apollinarian her-
> esy. The Church of the second Rome, Constantinople, has been
> hewn down by the axes of the Hagarenes. But this recent Church
> of the Third, New Rome, of thy sovereign Empire. . . shines in the
> whole universe more resplendent than the sun. . . . All the empires
> of the Orthodox Christian faith have come together in thy single
> Empire, thou are the sole Emperor of all the Christians in the whole
> universe. . . . For two Romes have fallen and the Third stands, a
> Fourth there shall never be.[73]

"Moscow was already surrounded by a halo."[74] The imperial
city came of age under leaders who became veritable monuments of
Greco-Byzantine traditions, moulded into shape by the formulations
and proddings of ecclesiastics reaching all the way back to the days
of Kievan Rus'. Abbot Joseph Sanin is a perfect example: "Though
in body the tsar is like all other men, yet in power he is like God."[75]

Though the image of the tsar and Russian Orthodoxy was destined to become even more awe-inspiring after overcoming domestic
and foreign conflicts in the decades ahead, an integral aspect of
Moscow's élan already included a firmly entrenched anti-Western,
anti-Latin spirit which was accepted and passed on to posterity. The
instruction of the Greeks was well learned in Moscow. "Since the
Russians are partisans of the Greek Church, they think they must
share the hostility that the Greek Church has borne the Latin for
many centuries."[76] Many have commented on the practice of the tsars
washing their hands after dealing with foreign diplomats and officials. "Ivan and Fyodor and Boris all had kept a basin handy when
receiving foreign ambassadors at court, to wash the befoulment sym-
bolically from their hands. Roman Catholics, Lutherans and Unitari-
ans were treated without distinction in the impenetrable sanctity of
Holy Russia."[77] Possevino commented on Ivan IV's ritual: "He
washes his hands as if to cleanse away sin."

The Muscovite state received added strength with the victory of the Josephites in their debate with Nil Sorsky and the Transvolga elders. The Josephites moved Orthodoxy toward a more rigorous ritualism and an even stronger working alliance with the state, at times calling in the secular arm to put down heresies with physical force. But the most elaborate ornamentation and embellishment of the secular and sacred characteristics of the Third Rome were saved for the metropolitanate of Macarius (1542–68). The *Stoglav* (Book of a Hundred Chapters) represented the codification of dogma, discipline, law, and ritual of the Orthodox Church agreed upon by a council in 1551. The *Domostroy* (Household Code) guided and reminded families of the very rudiments of everyday living. Orthodox hagiography received an added impetus with the compilation of the *Chetyi-Minei* (Menologion) and the standardization of the Church calendar. Finally, the heritage of Muscovite rulers was purported to extend without interruption to Prus, mythical brother of Emperor Augustus.[78]

While the glorification of the Muscovite state continued unabated, territories problems continued to mount in Catholic-Orthodox relations in the Polish-Lithuanian territories. The Orthodox struggled to survive in clearly unenviable conditions. Dependent on the patriarch of Constantinople who was at the mercy or caprice of the sultan, himself willing to sell the office to the highest bidder, the metropolitans became even more susceptible to the influence of the secular rulers of Poland and Lithuania. Naturally these same monarchs favored those most amenable to rapprochement with the West and Latin Rome.[79] Between 1534 and 1589 three of the five bigamist, another ill-educated, and the third a political appointment.[80]

All that kept the Western Orthodox from being destroyed through polonization and latinization was the struggle between the Polish and Lithuanians themselves. The real goal of Poland was "to unite Lithuania with Poland in one single monolithic government and swallow up all Lithuania and all the Russians in a Polish sea."[81] Conditions for the metropolitans in the East were scarcely better. Between 1505 and 1584 there were nine metropolitans; of these six were deposed, and one subsequently murdered.[82] Metropolitan Philip was strangled by the *oprichniki* for criticizing Ivan IV's unjust policies. In other words, the same church figures who helped raise the possibility of autocracy were the first to suffer for their efforts.

As Ivan IV declared: "I am free to bestow grace on my subjects and I am free to send them to the scaffold."[83]

That the hostility between Orthodox and Catholics continued at a high pitch on the official formal level is very evident during the reign of Ivan IV. In his debate with Prince Kurbsky this is everywhere evident. Non-Orthodox are ungodly and therefore enemies of the Muscovite state. Russia and Orthodoxy are the same thing. And he himself, as Orthodoxy's czar, has the task of securing the true faith against its inner enemies, by discipline and against its outer enemies by war.[84] In a polemical exchanges Ivan refers to Prince Kurbsky as the former

> boyar and adviser and voevoda of our autocratic state and of the true Christian Orthodox faith, but who is now the perjurer of the holy and life-giving Cross of the Lord and the destroyer of Christianity, the servant of those enemies of Christianity who have apostatized from the worship of the divine icons and trampled on all the sacred commandments and destroyed the holy temples and befouled and trampled on the sacred vessels and images.[85]

In 1564 and 1569 the Jesuits moved into Poland and Lithuania, spearheading the Counter Reformation and beginning a career that would place an indelible mark on the Russian consciousness for centuries to come. Offering the excellence of their education to all men, they were an instantaneous and extraordinary success.[86] Under Stephen Bathory (1576–86) and Sigismund III (1587–1632) who was educated by the Jesuits, the Society flourished in the Polish-Lithuanian Commonwealth. Peter Skarga, the Polish Canisius and Bossuet, figured prominently in this new campaign. Apologetical and polemical literature in Polish and Russian abounded in the battle for conversions.[87]

In 1581 Stephen Bathory's armies were ready to take the offensive against Pskov after checking the Muscovite attempt to expand on the Baltic. The battle as described in "The Story of Stephen Bathory's Campaign Against Pskov" is again another "holy war" against the enemies in the West. Bathory, for instance, is one who does not know the true God, burdened as he is with "lawless Latin heresies." With the heroic aid of valiant women of the city and wonder-working icons, the Lithuanians were repulsed.[88]

With Ivan IV's forces badly depleted and Poland and Sweden ready for a truce, Pope Gregory XIII sent the Jesuit Anthony Possevino to negotiate the settlement of Yam Zapolie. Though the war was stopped, the most sought-for goals of Rome and the emperor were lost. Ivan countenanced no inclination either to become the Emperor of the East or to spearhead a crusade against the Turks. Furthermore, there was no cooling of the hostility between Ivan and Rome. Indeed, the tsar engaged in debates with Possevino, ending in a shouting match in February 1582 in which Ivan reportedly exclaimed that the pope was no shepherd at all. "He is a wolf."[89] As for Isidore after Florence, so too for Possevino was the task unrealistic. Based on superficial knowledge and false hopes, Possevino was to establish commercial relations with Venice, work for the possibility of building a church and Russian soil, and getting permission for the Jesuits to settle in the capital of Moscow. Possevino went away empty-handed, while the Poles were doubtless chagrined at the negotiations, victory taken from their hands. Russia was the only party to profit from the truce.

Reunion efforts were simply out of the question. After Possevino had made references to the Florentine Union, Ivan retorted:

Why do you point out the Greeks to us; Greeks are no gospel to us; we believe not in the Greeks but in Christ. We received the Christian faith at the birth of the Christian church when Andrew, brother of the Apostle Peter, came to these parts on his way to Rome. Thus we in Moscow embraced the true faith at the same time that you did in Italy, and have kept it inviolate from then to the present day.[90]

In 1589 Moscow acquired the patriarchate. The event complemented the successful "gathering of the land" under Ivan III and Ivan the Terrible, a crowning achievement for bolstering once more the third Rome ideology. Under the last Rurik, Feodor, in the regency of Boris Godunov, Patriarch Joachim of Antioch consecrated Job patriarch of Russia on January 1589. Now a national, state church, Moscow could claim complete independence from its fallen mother, second Rome. Both state and church were thereby autocephalous and dependent on no other country for ideological support.

While Moscow achieved its ecclesiastical independence in the

East, movements were taking quite another turn in the West. Catholic influence was increasing in the South. Since the treaty of Union of Lublin in 1569, the Poles started moving in increasing numbers in Kiev and surrounding areas, exacerbating the religious problem. Jesuit influence continued to grow as well. After taking Polotsk in 1579, for instance, Stephen Bathory allowed a Jesuit college to be established there and turned all, except one, of the Orthodox churches and monasteries and landed estates over to the Jesuits.[91]

Movement for reunion once more became the major objective of Catholic parties and many of the Orthodox hierarchy in the West. Skarga's book, *The Unity of the Church of God*, expressed the sentiment for those ready to initiate talks and discussions. And in 1595 and 1596 at Brest, Lithuania, reunion was effected whereby roughly two thirds of the Orthodox living in the western borderlands joined the Church of Rome. The other third, including two bishops, resisted. Above all, the peasants resisted the union.

The religious settlement at Brest was destined to be a perilous one. An antisynod was held by the opponents of the union, guided by the spirit of Constantine Ostrogski, prince of Kiev Palatine, who declared the removal of Mikhail Ragoza, metropolitan of Kiev, and five other prominent members of the hierarchy. The antisynodal group considered the proponents of union anathema because "they had despised God and his Church."[92] The synod countered by deposing Balaban of Lvov and Kopystenski of Przemysl, the two Ruthenian bishops who sided with the opposition.

The bitter feelings and atrocities that followed were merely a continuation of the bad omens generated as far back as the Florentine union. Cyril Lucaris, later patriarch of Alexandria and Constantinople, barely escaped with his life. Nicephorus, vicar of the patriarch of Constantinople and opponent of the union, was strangled. Bishop Pociej of Brest, advocate of union and former Calvinist, whom Kartashev describes as not scrupling to slander, denounce, extort and arrest Orthodox priests and seize their property, was murdered.[93] Jehoshaphat, uniate bishop of Polotsk, was murdered and his body thrown into the river.[94]

In the fierce aftermath of the union, the Uniates were caught in the crossfire of both Latins and Orthodox. Dvornik refers to the "haughty treatment" they received from the Latins. Uniate bishops, for instance, were excluded from the Polish senate while laymen were obliged to pay double tithes, one to their own priests and another to Polish priests of the Latin rite. Pressures to latinize the Uniates and Orthodox alike destroyed any hopes for permanent reconciliation.[95]

The Time of Troubles

If Orthodox hostility to the Latin West and the work of the Jesuits did not become a fixation in the Russian consciousness at Brest, then it certainly did during the "Time of Troubles." Massive unrest prevailed on the Russian scene after the extinction of the Rurik line when Feodor died in 1598. Unleashed repression continued until the dyarchy of Michael Romanov and his father, Patriarch Philaret, in the second decade of the seventeenth century finally restored order. Feodor (1584–98), incompetent and looked on as an ordinary idiot by many, was dominated in his regency by Boris Godunov and Nikita Romanov. Boris continued to rule until his own death in 1605, but his reign was plagued by unrest and turmoil as well, notably in 1601–3 when widespread famine struck the country. Under these chaotic conditions, Moscow became easy prey for Poland and Sweden.

The crisis in the secular realm provided by the intrigue and revolt of the boyars and Cossacks who had long been held in check under Ivan IV, paralleled a traumatic experience in the religious sector. From 1602 on, the name 1591 *Dmitry* began to be heard more and more in Russian circles. The agents of Boris had supposedly assassinated this youngest son of Ivan in 1591. But now the resurrected heir suddenly appeared to reclaim his rightful rule. At this point, the Jesuits and Rome once more enter Russian affairs and convincingly win for themselves the centuries-old enmity and hostility of the Russian people.

Reinforced with Polish and Cossack soldiers, the false Dmitry, "a plaything of the Jesuits,"[96] marched on Moscow in late 1604. Though thoroughly demoralized with the first encounter, the unexpected death of Godunov and ensuing difficulties in reorganizing the government saved him. Conspiring against Feodor, the Shuiskis, Golitsins, and other boyars planned to use Dmitry to gain their own advantage. Thus Dmitry was swept into power, complete with military, court officials, and a new patriarch. According to Karamzin:

> Few monarchs were ever welcomed so joyously by the people as was the false Dmitry on the day of his triumphal entry into Moscow. Tales of the alleged miraculous rescue, memories of the terrible disasters of Godunov's reign, and the hope that Heaven, having restored the throne to the descendants of Vladimir, would also restore prosperity to Russia, inclined hearts favorably toward the young monarch, the favorite of fortune.[97]

But appearances were deceiving and the joyous triumph was short-lived, in spite of ingenious intrigues from all sides. The masses had long been taught to fear and dread foreigners, not to become contaminated by non-Russians and their false doctrines. For decades the fear of the Latin West had been expressed in the public prayers of the Orthodox Church. Special prayers were offered to keep Russia free from *Latinstvo*.[98] Now the Latins were in charge of Moscow itself. Worse yet, in the forefront of Dmitry's entourage were the Jesuits, notably Fathers Nicholas Czyrzowski and Andrew Lewicki. Using the power of the press, Possevino wrote pamphlets for publication in European capitals supporting Dmitry's legitimacy. Capitalizing on the masses' religious reverence for icons, pictures of Dmitry were printed for widespread circulation.

Once more Rome's plans went awry. Dmitry outwardly professed Orthodoxy, and it was clear enough that he had no intentions to convert Russia for the Vatican. As a result he did not please the Poles who helped sweep him into power. Neither did he please the Russians. They were aghast at his behavior. "On the throne he resembled more a tramp than a king." He was not a religious man, scorning the accustomed fasts; he took no siestas; he walked through the streets as a commoner. His wife Marina and her entourage of Catholic priests, moreover, made his rule even less acceptable. In a word, he did not act like a Russian tsar.[99] In May 1606 Dmitry was dead, struck down by the boyars. In complete disgrace, his body was dragged through the streets, and his remains were shot through a cannon.

The Image of Dmitry

The bitterness and almost fanatical hatred that developed because of the Polish-Catholic activities in Moscow and Russia are graphically exposed in the work of the monk Avraamy Palitsyn of the Holy Trinity-St. Sergius Monastery. The monk describes Dmitry as being possessed by the evil spirit, thereby "winning over the entire universe, the entirety of Europe; and even the Pope of Rome."[100] Besides corrupting nuns and pious monks, Dmitry promises that he will "bring entire Russia under the blessing of the Antichrist, thus delivering all Russians to eternal death through the abomination of the Catholic Communion."[101]

Pushkin's *Boris Godunov* best preserves the diabolical overtones of the Romish-Jesuitical plot. In his recreation when Dmitry tells a Catholic priest in Cracow that in two years all the Eastern Church will recognize Peter's Vicar in Rome. Pushkin has the priest reply: "May Saint Ignatius aid thee when other times shall come." Encouraging Dmitry to guard this holy secret, the priest continues: "Religious duty bids us often to dissemble before the blabbing world. The people judge your words, your deeds; God only sees your motives."[102] Even Dmitry boasts how he deceived "the brainless Poles;"[103] he comments on the supposedly machiavellian tactics of *Latinstvo*: "Neither king, nor pope, nor nobles trouble whether my words be true, whether I be Dmitry or another. What care they? But I provide a pretext for revolt and war; and this is all they need. . . ."[104]

Alexander Sumarokov's version of Dmitry the Impostor capitalizes on another issue evoked during the Time of Troubles: the power of the papacy. Here the pope is depicted as believing himself a sort of God on earth. "Some call him patriarch—among his equals, first; but not the world's sole judge; not the highest prince, not God. The Pope must realize men are not witless cattle."[105] Commenting on the treacherous motives of the Impostor, Sumarokov has Dmitry say: "But Russia's honor must descend to utter darkness. My armies will accept the Pope father of fathers; for him will I subdue the Church with tools of war."[106] Making the image of Dmitry even more damaging, instead of being set on by boyar conspirators, Dmitry is pictured stabbing himself, gasping: "Go, then, my soul, to hell and be forever captive! If only with me now the whole world too would perish!"[107]

The End of the Troubles

Russian woes did not cease with the death of Dmitry. Nor did the

Poles give up. In 1610 they again controlled Moscow. Sigismund even made plans to become tsar himself. The Russian Church proved a rallying factor once more as Patriarch Germogen (1606–12) provided moral leadership until a Russian tsar could be chosen. In 1611, however, Smolensk fell after a siege of twenty months. And by 1612 Russian fortunes looked even more ominous. Again in 1618 the Poles marched on Moscow. But with the Armistice of Deulino in the same year, the Polish threat was weakened.[108] Deulino signaled the beginning of the end of Polish control and influence in Russia. Polish military losses, moreover, meant the defeat of Catholicism since its cause was so intrinsically related with Polish arms Any hopes left for reunion were simply unrealistic.

From 1619 on, when Nikita Romanov [Philaret] returned from Polish captivity, the dyarchy of Michael and Nikita jointly ruled Russia, sharing the title of "Great Sovereign." Nikita's policies in church affairs reflected the popular mood of Russia society after experiencing the horrors of the false Dmitries and the "Time of Troubles." To keep Orthodoxy uncontaminated by Western heresy, Philaret attempted to build an ideological wall between the West and Russia. Indicative of this viewpoint, Michael issued a ukase in 1629 forbidding Orthodox believers to serve or work under the non-Orthodox.[109] To eliminate any possible deviations in the orthodoxy of the believer, Philaret ordered Latin converts settling in Muscovy to be rebaptized before acceptance in the Russian Church. Sometimes even Orthodox relocating in Russian territory were also rebaptized, especially if they had not been previously christened by immersion.[110]

When Wladyslaw IV succeeded Sigismund in 1632, he granted concessions to Orthodox living in the Polish-Lithuanian territories, the most important of which was the right to have an Orthodox metropolitan in Kiev. Peter Mogila was elected to the post in 1633, and his leadership guided Orthodoxy on a new path. By updating the intellectual standards of the Orthodox clergy, for instance, Mogila enhanced the possibility of Russian Orthodox to counter the attractive educational and propaganda projects of the Jesuits and western clergy. Mogila's leadership was especially timely, as many Orthodox were dying in Polish-Lithuanian territories without the sacraments; others were deprived of their own churches. Guarantees of religious freedom were not observed.[111] Under Mogila Orthodoxy was able to survive and begin to rebuild its position. But relations between

Catholics, Orthodox, and Uniates remained touchy. Runciman, for example, recalls the wild stories about the Jesuits which continued to circulate. One story concerns a Ruthenian princess "whom they had converted and then persuaded to exhume the rotting corpse of her father so as to have him baptized in the Latin rite."[112]

At the death of Sigismund, the Cossacks presented a petition to the Polish Senate for more political autonomy in their territories and a greater say in the election of the Polish king. But they were rebuffed; from that point on, the political-religious exacerbation grew in intensity in the Ukraine, culminating in rapprochement between the Ukraine and Muscovy. Political and religious enmity between the Zaporozhie Cossacks and the Poles reached a fierce state in the 1640s. In the Ukraine the gentry and ruling class were hunted with dogs and had their houses burned to the ground. The clergy was decimated. "Every Uniate or Catholic priest who could be caught was hung up before his own high altar, along with a Jew and a hog.[113]

Led by Hetman Bogdan Khmelnitsky, the Cossacks succeeded in wearing down the Poles during intermittent military campaigns that brought havoc and devastation to both sides. New concessions from Polish King John Casimir included promises to withdraw the Jews, Jesuits, and Polish troops from Cossack lands and allow more autonomy for Orthodoxy. In 1649 Khmelnitsky called for the complete abolishment of the Uniate Church in the Ukraine and the closing down of all the Catholic churches.

An interesting document of these times, *The Travels of Macarius*, indicates the bitter hatred between Catholic and Orthodox. Archdeacon Paul of Aleppo praises Khmelnitsky for delivering "millions of Orthodox believers from the accursed Poles." He then explains why he calls the Poles accursed:

> Because they have shown themselves more vile and wicked than even the worshipers of idols by their cruelty to Christians, thinking to extinguish the name of Orthodoxy and to make them to obey the Pope, as they do. God perpetuate the Empire of the Turks! For they take their impost and enter into no account of religion, to their subjects Christians or Nazarenes, Jews or Samaritans; whereas these accursed Poles, not content with taking taxes and tithes from their Christian subjects, subjected them to the enemies of Christ, the Jews, who did not allow them to build churches or leave them any educated priests."[114]

The Archdeacon also denounces the Poles for the systematic murder of Orthodox hierarchy over the past forty years, including a metropolitan along with eleven of his bishops and priests, "roasting them on the fire with iron tongs, thinking thus to terrify and subdue them."[115] Paul then heaps praises on Khmelnitsky, the holy warrior for the Orthodox faith. "Truly God is with Thee, Khmelnitsky! He raised thee up to deliver his people as Moses delivered Israel, so thou has destroyed the filthy Poles with thy depopulating sword!"[116] According to Paul over ninety towns and castles were taken over by Khmelnitsky while his army displayed "its zeal for the Orthodox Church by slaughtering Jews, Armenians, and Poles and throwing their children, packed in barrels into the Dnieper."[117]

By the Treaty of Andrusovo in 1667, the Poles lost large areas of the Ukraine. According to one of the thirty-three articles of the armistice, Russian Orthodox residing in Poland and Roman Catholics in Russia were not to be persecuted or harmed in any way.[118]

Though Muscovy was successful in reclaiming old borders disputed with foreign powers, she had to deal with a new crisis on the domestic ecclesiastical front. Reform-minded individuals had stirred the country by midcentury, notably under Patriarch Nikon (1652–58). During his reign the power of the Church reached its apogee, thereafter only to be weakened and damaged. One of Nikon's major goals was to lead Russia out of her cultural and religious isolation by forging closer relationships with the Greek Orthodox. But Nikon's reforms in textual criticism, liturgy, and ritual were challenged by the staunch defenders of tradition, especially Ivan Neronov, N. F. Kapterev, and Archpriest Avvakum. Nikon was castigated for praising the laws of the foreigners and approving their customs. Such openness did not include Catholicism, for Nikon had little or no sympathy for Latin Rome. When Nikon noticed some Latin tendencies in certain icon paintings, he became indignant. "With characteristic display of temperament he threw these icons on the stone floor of the church, pierced the eyes of the saints and disregarding the pleas of the Tsar ordered them burned, while he called out the names of their owners."[119] After the trial and downfall of Nikon, the Russian Church, for all practical purposes, lost her formerly exalted place in Russian affairs. As the Council of 1667 declared, "The Tsar has power to rule the patriarch and all other priests, for there must not be two heads in one autocratic state, but the royal power should be supreme."[120]

The End of the Russian Patriarchate

Up to the time of Peter the Great, no Catholic church was permitted in Moscow, and no clergy were allowed to live there permanently. But in the eighties the Jesuits had a little colony there, serving as chaplains in the various embassies. By 1685 they acquired a house in the German *Sloboda*. Once established, according to Dmitry Tolstoy, they attracted Russian children to their schools, dabbled in politics, and engaged in spy activities. They were clearly dangerous because of their "fanaticism and propaganda."[121] Worried by the continuing effects of Raskol, Patriarch Joachim (1674–90) explained to the young tsars Peter and John the dangers ahead. He demanded the expulsion of the Jesuits stating that "Rome had apostatized in separating itself from the apostolic church," and that the Jesuits would only seduce Orthodox believers. Orthodoxy made another comeback in 1687 when Constantinople's Patriarch Dionysius concurred with other patriarchs in confirming the Russian desire to reincorporate under its own jurisdiction those Russian Orthodox living in the Ukraine and Polish-Lithuanian territories.

One of the few bright aspects of this period regarding Orthodox-Catholic relations involved General Patrick Gordon, a Scottish military leader who served under the tsars for almost forty years, 1661–99. The Jesuit P. Emiliani wrote that "no one had done more for the Catholic cause in Russia than Gordon and his family." Sofiya Buksgevden calls him "the official Champion of Catholicism."[122]

When Patriarch Adrian (1690–1700) shared little of Peter's enthusiasm for importing ideas from the West, Peter did not appoint a successor to the vacancy. Instead he gave the title of "custodian of the patriarchal throne" to Stephen Javorsky, bishop of Riazan and Moscow, until a new form of ecclesiastical governing structure could be arranged.

The real clerical power behind Peter's throne was Theofan Prokopovich (1681–1736). Considered one of the best educated men of his time, Prokopovich was born in Kiev, studied in Poland and Rome, but returned to Russia with a bitter hatred for Catholicism. At the battle of Poltava, Theofan referred to Catholics as "the servants of the Devil." In a sermon in honor of Menshikov, he exhorted the Orthodox "to destroy the thrice-cursed union which has penetrated the holy churches in the Polish states and restore to its own rites the piety driven out from thence, to cast out the wolves who walk in sheep's clothing and introduce true and good shepherds."[123]

Prokopovich, archbishop of Novgorod in 1720, became the first vice-president of the Holy Synod and compiler of the Spiritual Regulation by which the patriarchate was officially abolished. Under this new dispensation the Russian Church became a department of the state. Prokopovich, second to none, glorified the role of his tsar, declaring that "among so many earthly kings there is only one who follows Christ in truth, alone he shines not only with the radiance of majesty but also with the light of Orthodoxy."[124] According to Kartashev, "Teofan was Peter's living academy for all questions on church and state. Teofan became the brain of Peter."[125]

Before he had to deal with the complexities of military strategy, Peter went out of his way to express an ecumenical openmindedness during his tour of the West between 1697 and 1699. He attended Mass, intimated that the union of the churches was not an absolute impossibility and even drank to the health of the Holy Father. But these were only diplomatic pleasantries. While visiting a monastery of the Basilians at Polotskoa July 11, 1705, Peter paused at a statue of one of the martyrs of the order, Josaphat Kuncewicz. The Uniate archbishop of Polotsk was killed by dissidents during a riot on November 12, 1623. Josaphat was represented with a hatchet sticking in his skull. Peter inquired who was responsible for putting the saint to death. When the monks replied that the "schismatics" did it, Peter pulled out his sword and killed one priest, Father Kozikowski, on the spot while his officers made short work of three others. The monastery was sacked and the church was used as a military store. Peter's account of the incident included the charge that the monks worked with the enemies of the empire, failed to receive him with proper ceremony, and answered his query about the saint by saying: "That is St. Josaphat, who was killed by your coreligionists, heretics, apostates and persecutors like yourselves."[126] In the post-Petrine period, antiwestern and antiforeign sentiment rose appreciably during Anna's rule. "But the man whose name became a byword for all that was detestable in the rule of foreigners, the man believed to be the real power behind Anna's throne, was Ernst Johann Biron, who did not occupy any official position in the government."[127]

While Peter was embarking on his "westernization" of Russia, he permitted a modest Jesuit activity in Moscow. But since this permission was granted in good part through the gracious assistance of

Peter's half-sister Sophia, the Jesuits were turned out after her death. In 1740 under Tsarina Anne, the Jesuits were allowed to return.[128]

Hostilities between Orthodox and Catholics reached another crest under Catherine the Great. She initiated the triple partitions of Poland in 1772, 1793, and 1795, and thus gave eastern Catholicism a blow from which it never recovered. This was the ultimate triumph of Orthodoxy and the Russian Empire over the ancient and most bitter enemy, in part, retaliation for the lack of political and religious freedom of those dissidents living in the old Polish-Lithuanian Commonwealth.The only compensation, paradoxically, to one branch of Latin Catholicism belongs to the Jesuits. Catherine revoked the proscription of Peter the Great and drew up working conditions for the Jesuits in the old Polish territories, allowing them to survive the order of suppression as mandated by Clement XIV in 1773. Roughly two hundred Jesuits manned schools and colleges in these territories with headquarters in St. Petersburg. Though these conditions continued under Catherine's successor, Jesuit successes hastened the day of their own demise, for a ukase dated December 25, 1815, by Alexander expelled the Jesuits from Russia proper. On March 13, 1820, Alexander extended his 1815 ban to include the entire Russian Empire.[129]

The eighteenth century in Russia was a crucial period, for the intellectuals desperately desired to come to terms with their country's destiny, and quite naturally this involved an appraisal of the "Latin West." One of the most representative of these men was Denis Fonvizin (1745-92) writer and aide to Catherine. His two comedies, *The Brigadier* and *Adolescent*, but most especially his *Letters from France*, betray this effort to deal with a most agonizing question. In his trips abroad Fonvizin poured out a black picture of European life in letters to his sister Feodosia Ivanovna and to Peter Panin, the brother of Count Panin.

In the main, Fonvizin's critical barbs for the Catholic Church are more satiric and comic than destructive. He does observe, though, that "the power of the clergy in France is such that the most prominent among them have no fear of losing it no matter what temptations they succumb to. Prelates publicly keep wenches and there is nothing more shameful then the life led by French abbots."[130] In Europe, moreover, "the bad hits you in the eyes," and one must search and hunt down the good.[131] Fonvizin went so far as to say that if any of his fellow countrymen became disillusioned or alienated with their own homeland, they should be sent to France for the "cure."[132] Gallomania was also flaunted in I. B. Kniazhnin's *Misfortune from a Coach* where we have the following dialog:

> Firiulin: We're nothing compared to the French.
>
> Jester: It was worth traveling to France to bring back just contempt, not only for one's fellow countrymen, but for one's self.
>
> Firiulin: To unfortunate people like us who have returned from France to this savage country one pleasure has remained, and that is that after making a decent turnover on this Russian trash one can get some respectable French thing.[133]

Paul and Conciliation with the West

Meanwhile under the new Tsar Paul, relations with the Catholic Church were more than cordial. The Jesuits especially were welcomed and treated with admiration. In fact, sensational rumors circulated concerning Paul's religious attitudes when he assumed the title of Grand Master of the Knights of Malta in 1798. Paul even offered the pope asylum from revolutionary Europe. While welcoming Catholic propagandists, Paul quarreled with Plato, the metropolitan of Moscow and treated Gabriel, metropolitan of St. Petersburg, with decided coldness. Perhaps Paul was ready to issue a decree subordinating Russian Orthodoxy to Catholicism. Only a premature death spoiled this plan.[134] Another sensational rumor had Paul making designs on the papacy itself.[135]

Though Catholicism continued to find favor on the official level under Paul's successor, the Napoleonic invasion evoked such antiforeignism that everything non-Russian became highly suspect. In the upheaval Catholics lost favor, and the Jesuits in particular lost their privileged place of honor in Alexander's regime. France, the grand symbol of Latin Catholic Europe, recalled all that was dangerous and evil. Count Fyodor Rostopchin (1763–1826), military governor of Moscow during the French invasion, epitomized popular sentiment against this trespass upon Russian soil: "Let us destroy the remaining enemy forces. Let us bury them in Holy Russia. . . . He [the tsar] relies upon Almighty God, on the God of the Russian Land. . . . He alone is the anointed of God. . . He is the Father, we are

His children, while the evil Frenchman is the unbaptized [nekreshchenyi] enemy."[136]

The Return to Europe

By the nineteenth century few problems disturbed the Russian consciousness more than its relationship with the West. Now awestruck, now condescending and self-sufficient, both official government policy and private intellectuals struggled with this tradition of ambivalence, this oscillation of attitudes. Above all, Russian intellectuals wanted to put their own self-image and the Russian concept of Europe in proper perspective.

Eight centuries of Russian life had made one thing clear: Russia and Orthodoxy were wedded. Russia identified itself with its church. And a spirited animosity toward the Latin Church was an essential characteristic of Orthodoxy as inherited from the Greeks. Since the Rus' Church and the Rus' State were copies of the Byzantine Church and State, their heir, the Russian nation, was a copy of the Byzantine nation. The Orthodox faith could do without Russia, but the converse is out of the question: there can be no Russia without the Orthodox faith.[137] Until the Mongol invasion, seventeen of twenty-three Metropolitans holding Russian sees were Greeks; this was long after Russians predominated over the Greeks and Bulgarians among both monks and local priests.[138] This was an inescapable feature which had been developing between East and West long before 1054. Old Roman universalism broke up into Greek, Russian, and European nationalism and factionalism.

The Mongolian occupation, which made the Rus' church safe from the pressures of the popes,[139] only served to virtually wall off Russia from the West and allowed the deeply embedded mutual mistrust to deepen between Rus' and Rome. Moreover, Rus' could rightly claim that the West cared little for her plight during the Mongol siege, for, from her viewpoint, the West doubly jeopardized the sad straits of Rus' by making incursions on the borderlands to the west. This was the second factor in deepening the wounds of separation. In the process Poland became the symbol of the dangerous, heretical West, especially of Latin Rome, attempting to foist a religious creed on an already Christian country through force of arms.

The third Rome ideology of Rus' reflected the chaotic conditions in Constantinople and a shaky situation in Europe. This was the third factor naturally following upon the previous two which served to instill and deepen religious hatred. Rus' had inherited the mission of showing the way to Christians of East and West in Europe. "Psychologists and anthropologists have shown the universality of most myths, founded as they are on human insecurity, on a universal need to justify and in some sense to explain away reality. But while all societies manifest basic and similar fears and needs, each expresses them in unique form, according to its particular history and circumstances."[140]

After the fifteenth century when ideologies became fixed or crystallized, the three Romes continued to live in relative religious isolation, developing their own cultures under new social circumstances, tempers, and national consciousnesses. Xenophobia is a favorite friend of nationalism and each of the three formerly united peoples went their own paths, save when expediency called for occasional compromises or friendly relations. In its own isolation, mainly as a result of the Mongol occupation and its aftereffects, Russia shared few of the benefits of the Renaissance and Reformation. It had no strong spirit of rationalistic inquiry; it produced no Thomas Aquinas or Calvin. The intellectual tradition of the West passed it by.

The Time of Troubles was a lasting memorial of Latin casuistry in the Russian mind. Religious fanaticism on both sides continued to remain rooted on both sides. Shcherbatov's (1733–90) comment on the pace of Russia's modernization is attributable to both sides of the curtain: "The Russian people used to be devout to the point of fanaticism, regarding Christians of all other confessions as infidels; for example, it was held to be a sin and a dishonor to have visited Germans in the sloboda."[141]

Toward the waning years of the eighteenth century and the beginning of the nineteenth century, Russian intellectuals, breaking away from official, formal ideology, began to question their destiny in the light of their relationship with the West. Operating in a more highly secular vein, they were troubled by some inescapable reflections. "To look back on their past, which still surrounded them at every step, as evil and barbaric would have been a denial of their national identity. The impossibility of such a denial was forcefully brought home to them by the condescension with which most Westerners wrote about Russia."[142]

The beginning of the nineteenth century and the victory of Napoleon, paradoxically, brought an even stronger flood of ideas and experiences from the West. Russian thought and culture were once more ambushed by the Western nations. Toward the end of the Napoleonic war there were in Russia roughly 400 Jesuits who "were valued not only as a bulwark against revolution but as a source of skilled personnel for everything from education (for which purposes Catherine had welcomed them) to the making of confections (for which Paul particularly valued the general of the order)."[143] Although this new influence was curtailed during the later years of Alexander I, the doors had already beep forced open too wide to close again.

The Westernizers

The utter failure of the Decembrist revolt and the increasingly arbitrary rule of Nicolas I insured that critical views of the entire Russian system would burst onto the scene with greater rapidity. Inevitably, comparisons were made between Russia and Europe. One Russian intellectual who brooded over this accursed question was Peter Chaadaev. His agonizing response to this burning question "set the tone, it struck the dominant notes which were echoed by every major Russian writer up to and beyond the Revolution."[144]

For Chaadaev the only true culture was found in the West; Catholicism was the fruition and synthesis of western civilization. In his famous *Philosophical Letters*, Chaadaev unleashed one of the most scandalous criticisms of his country. "We have never walked hand in hand with other nations. We do not belong to any of the great families of mankind, either to the West or to the East, we do not have the tradition of either. We exist as if beyond the limits of time and as if we were never touched by the universal education of humanity."[145]

Chaadaev castigated what he felt to be the total lack of success in Russia's past. At first there was a

> brutal barbarism, then crude superstition, after that fierce, degrading foreign domination by strangers whose spirit was later inherited by the national government—that is the sad history of our youth. . . .
> If the barbarian hordes which convulsed the world had not passed through the country in which we live before precipitating themselves upon the West, we would scarcely have furnished a chapter in world history. In order to call attention to ourselves, we had to expand from the Bering Strait to the Oder.[146]

The Slavophiles

Chaadaev was only a minority of one. But his views served as a catalyst for his contemporaries and those to come, for he questioned the path of Russian history, philosophy, and theology, in essence the entire scope of Russian civilization down to its very roots. Chaadaev did not have to wait long for an answer. V. F. Odoevsky came to the defense of Russia, stating that what Chaadaev said of Russia he would say of Europe and vice versa. In a West that was perishing, there was nothing left but an "old enfeebled Europe."

> Religious feeling in the West? It would have been forgotten long ago if it had not been for its external language, which remained as an adornment, like Gothic architecture, or hieroglyphics or furniture, or for the selfish ends of people who use this language as a novelty. The Western Church is now a political arena; its religious feeling, a conventional sign of small parties. . . . We must save not only the *body* of Europe, but her *soul* as well! . . . We are placed on the border of two worlds: the past and the future; we are young and fresh; we are not privy to the crimes of the old Europe. . . . Nine out of ten so-called Roman Catholics believe neither in the infallibility of the Pope nor in the honesty of the Jesuits, and yet all of them are ready to fight with knives for both. We have become so accustomed to lies that these phenomena do not seem strange to us.[147]

Odoevsky was only the first of many to challenge Chaadaev's views and offer a full size rebuttal. Thereafter the Slavophiles, notably Khomyakov, I. V. Kireevsky, Y. F. Samarin and the brothers Aksakov, rose to the occasion as well. Flourishing especially from 1840 to 1860, the Slavophiles often idealized Orthodoxy and the patriarchal form of peasant society, especially the village commune. They adhered to a Russia-first attitude with full appreciation of Russia's cultural heritage: the tried and the tested.

A. S. Khomyakov (1804–60) was the recognized spokesman for the Slavophiles. He contrasted his own philosophy of complete freedom for the individual as possible within the framework of a free community of faith, reason, and will, with Western social systems. He characterized the latter as attempts to escape the responsibility of freedom by flight to a realm of necessity, embodied in the authoritarian bureaucratic state and the Roman Catholic Church.

Khomyakov dwelled with particular emphasis on the distinctions between Catholicism, Orthodoxy, and Protestantism. In his estimation Latinism represented unity without freedom; Protestantism represented freedom without unity; Orthodoxy reconciled the two. Obey and believe says Rome. Be free and create your own faith says Protestantism. Let us love one another and confess in the Trinity says Orthodoxy.[148]

Khomyakov believed that "Western Europe developed not under the influence of Christianity, but under the influence of Latinism, that is, of Christianity interpreted one-sidedly as the law of external unity."[149] Therefore he saw nothing but doom for the West. Writing in a letter to A. N. Popov on March 17, 1848, he declared that "the papacy of Gregory is going the way of Charlemagne's empire—to the historical archives. There, after them will follow Protestantism and Catholicism. The field is free. Orthodoxy comes into world prominence. The Slav nation come into world prominence. The hour is great.[150] Khomyakov saw no other salvation but in Orthodoxy. Mankind had only two choices: Orthodoxy or infidelity.[151]

Ivan V. Kireevsky (1806–56) reproached the West and the Roman Church for its excessive rationalism and "system building." On matters of faith he writes that

> Rome gave preference to abstract syllogism over sacred tradition, which is the repository of the common consciousness of the whole Christian world, and which holds it together in a living, indissoluble unity. This preference for syllogism over tradition was actually the only condition for the separate and independent rise of Rome. For how else could the Roman Church have become divorced from the Universal Church? It separated from it only because it wished to introduce new dogmas into the faith, dogmas unknown to Church tradition and born of the accidental deductions of the logic of Western peoples. . . . Hence we had scholasticism with all of its speculative refinements, which sought endlessly to reconcile the demands of reason with the affirmations of the hierarchy, and in so doing constantly drifted away from them into a countless multitude of heretical systems and interpretations.[152]

Kireevsky drew up a long line of contrasts which he felt epitomized the different patterns of development between the two civilizations: between the West's abstract logic and the East's integrity of spirit; external, dead unity, and living essence; a church mingled with state affairs, and a church aloof from worldly institutions and purposes; scholasticism, law learning and purity of tradition; turbulence, and steadfastness of basic convictions; ostentatious luxury—even artificiality—and simplicity of needs and moral fortitude; tendencies to effeminacy and fancifulness, and healthy integrity of mental faculties. Kireevsky concludes his summary of the divergence of these two traditions by writing that "if what we have set forth is correct, *dichotomy* and *integrity, ratiocination* and *intelligence* are the ultimate expressions of Western European and ancient Russian culture."[153]

Konstantin Aksakov (1817–60) also saw a black future for the West. He wrote that "the *soul is on the wane* in the West; it is being replaced by the improvement of state forms and police-enforced public order; conscience is being replaced by regulation."[154] Aksakov offered his own explanation for this phenomenon. "The reason why the West has developed legalism was that it felt in itself a lack of truth."[155] His brother, Ivan (1823–86), outspoken and often at odds with the official government, struck out at the papacy of the West.

> The Roman curia. . . . embodies all the spiritual essence of the West. . . . Slavdom has no greater enemy than the Papacy, because it is contrary to the very essence of the Slav spiritual nature . . . Orthodox Christianity does not impair the prestige of any nationality; with Rome, however, it is different. . . . The Roman Church is imbued throughout with a one-sidedness. . . . It is nothing but the West itself—Rome aggrandizing itself into a position of universal significance.[156]

Yuri F. Samarin (1819–76), one of the most ardent Slavophiles and active in practical politics, continued the development of the slavophile position with his ideas on the nature of the Church-State relationships. Notable for his lengthy correspondence with the Russian Jesuit Martynov, he referred to Jesuitism as "the last and the most legitimate offspring of Latinism.[157]

Samarin focused his attention on the suppression of the individual in the Catholic Church:

> In Latinism the individual is lost in the church; he loses all his rights and becomes as if dead, a small component particle of a whole. The historical task of Latinism has consisted in extracting the idea of unity, understood as power. . . from the living Church, and in transforming this unity between faith and love into a legal principle, with the members of the church becoming the subjects of its head.[158]

Samarin mentions the general trend of the discussions among fellow Slavophiles.

We used to argue about the relation between Orthodoxy, Latinism and Protestantism. Is Orthodoxy the undifferentiated and primitive form of Christianity from which the other and higher expressions of religion have arisen through the process of evolution or is Orthodoxy the unchangeable fullness of religious truth, whilst Christianity in the West has been drawn to opposite poles under the influence of Latin and German traditions?[159]

The Slavophiles represented the most consistent and persistent position against the West and the Catholic Church. Their strong influence was felt the longest. Two other Russians, from among many who held similar attitudes toward the Catholic Church were Alexander Herzen (1812–70) and Nicholas Danilevsky (1822–85). Herzen wrote of the utter unsuitability of Catholicism to the Slav temperament.

Catholicism, so alien to the Slavonic genius, has a shattering effect on it. When the Bohemians no longer had the strength to resist Catholicism, they were crushed; in the Poles, Catholicism has developed that mystical exaltation which keeps them perpetually in the world of dreams. If they are not under the direct influence of the Jesuits, they either create some idol for themselves, or give themselves up to the influence of some visionary instead of working for freedom.[160]

Danilevsky made perhaps one of the most caustic remarks about the differences between East and West: "And, on the other hand, is not the distinction between Catholicism and Protestantism greater than that between Catholicism and Orthodoxy. . . ? This can be answered very briefly, for the distinction of truth from a lie is infinite and two lies are always less distinct from one another than either of them from truth."[161]

Conclusion

By the second half of the nineteenth century, when Dostoevsky began to make his major literary breakthroughs, polemics between East and West polluted the air. Dostoevsky by then had already breathed deeply in the slavophile tradition. Shortly he would rise to the occasion and devote an important part of his remaining years to answering the challenge of Chaadaev himself and wrestle with the entire problem of Russia's relationship with the "Latin West."

TWO

DOSTOEVSKY: PROPHET OF RUSSIAN ORTHODOXY

Introduction

Writers flourished in nineteenth century Russia; few countries rival their prolific output and influence. Stimulated by agonizing questions about trends in domestic and foreign policy, they rivaled one another in advancing their views before the Russian public. Many hoped to thrust Russia to an unparalleled place of honor in history; to do this, they claimed special inspiration in forging their particular positions on the great questions of the day. Pushkin (1799–1837) described his calling and duty as a poet in the words of the call of Isaiah. For Lermontov (1814–41) too, the poet was a prophet. The tragedy of Gogol's life (1809–52) was that he felt himself the oracle of God. Dostoevsky shared this conviction.[1]

"Prophet, prophet!" shouted the crowd listening to Dostoevsky's address on Pushkin on June 8, 1880. From that day on, the word *prophet* has been linked with the name of Dostoevsky. Vladimir Solovyov particularly underlined the prophetic strain in Dostoevsky.[2] Dostoevsky saw himself as a prophet for his times. His ideas gained him the position of prominent spokesman in the second half of the nineteenth century, for his voice both announced the mood and force of a powerful sector of Russia's historical direction, and modified the character, personality, and temperament of his fellow Russians.

Dostoevsky's Life and Works

It is important to bear in mind the key importance of the relationship of Dostoevsky's personal life to his writing from the beginning of his career.

> The life and work of Dostoevsky are inseparable. He 'lived in literature.' It was his life's concern and his tragic fate. In all of his works he resolved the enigma of his personality; he spoke only of those things which he himself had personally experienced. Dostoevsky was always drawn to confession as an artistic form. His works unfold before us as one vast confession, as the integral revelation of his universal spirit.[3]
>
> In the case of both Tolstoy and Dostoevsky . . . their works are so bound up with their lives, with the personality of each author that we cannot speak of the one without the other. Before studying them as artists, thinkers, or preachers, we must know what manner of men they are.[4]

Berdyayev declares that "Dostoevsky is drunk with ideas," that his heroes are embodied ideas who "open their mouths to develop their ideological dialectic," often enough the very ideas of Dostoevsky himself.[5] A careful perusal of the letters and life of Dostoevsky will discover the most basic and detailed parallels with the creative works of the author. The ideas and thought patterns of one are reflected in the other.

Dostoevsky's Youth

The second of eight children, Fyodor Dostoevsky was born on October 30, 1821, in a Moscow hospital for the poor where his father worked as a physician. Although his mother was Russian, his ancestors on his father's side were of Lithuanian lineage; indeed at one time, they were Roman Catholics.[6] Important for later consideration is a remark of Dostoevsky: "I was only ten when I already knew virtually all the principal episodes in Russian history—from Karamzin whom, in the evenings, father used to read aloud to us."[7]

The doctor, a heavy drinker with a highly volatile nature, regularly accompanied his children to the historic spots and cathedrals of Moscow. Church attendance was easy for the family, for they were only a few steps from the Chapel of Saints Peter and Paul.

Others in the family circle influenced his religious life. The family made annual pilgrimages to the Trinity–St. Sergius Monastery.[8] His mother, a gentle and devoted woman, taught her children to read and write, using episodes from the Old and New Testaments as a textbook. A Russian Orthodox deacon frequented the household, and expounded on the stories in *The Holy History of the Old and New Testament*.[9] Dostoevsky especially cherished the memory of his nurse, Alyona Frolovna; he appreciated her devoted attention to his well-being. When three years old he learned one of his favorite prayers from her: "I place all my hope in Thee, Mother of God preserve me under Thy protection."[10]

Dostoevsky summarized his early religious history: "I descended from a pious Russian family. . . . We, in our family, have known the Gospel almost ever since our earliest childhood. . . . Every visit to the Kremlin and the Moscow cathedral was, to me, something solemn." (*Diary of a Writer* 1:152.)

Dostoevsky saved his most poignant commentary on early religious experiences for his last work, *The Brothers Karamazov*, where he portrayed the youth of the Elder Zossima:

> With my memories of home I count, too, my memories of the Bible, which, child as I was, I was very eager to read at home. I had a book of Scripture history then with excellent pictures, called 'A Hundred and Four Stories from the Old and New Testament,' and I learned to read from it. I have it lying on my shelf now, I keep it as a precious relic of the past. But even before I learned to read, I remember first being moved to devotional feeling at eight years old. My mother took me along to mass (I don't remember where my brother was at the time) on the Monday before Easter. It was a fine day, and I remember today, as though I saw it now, how the incense rose from the censer and softly floated upwards and, overhead in the cupola, mingled in rising waves with the sunlight that streamed in at the little window. I was stirred by the sight, and for the first time in my life I consciously received the seed of God's word in my heart. A youth came

out into the middle of the church carrying a big book, so large that at the time I fancied he could scarcely carry it. He laid it on the reading desk, opened it, and began reading, and suddenly for the first time I understood something read in the church of God. In the land of Ur, there lived a man, righteous and God-fearing, and he had great wealth. . . .(*Brothers Karamazov*, 346–47.)

In a letter from Ems in June 1875, Dostoevsky recounted to his wife the powerful impression that the Scriptures made on him, in this particular case, the Book of Job: "This book Anna, it's strange—is one of the first which made an impression on me in life, I was just then only a little boy!" (*Pis'ma* 3:177.)

Dostoevsky's mother died February 27, 1838. Shortly thereafter the young Fyodor and his brother, Mikhail, were sent to an army engineering school in St. Petersburg. Dostoevsky spent over five years of his young life there, building plans for the future. In June 1839, Dostoevsky's father was murdered by his own serfs who resented their master's irascible and capricious treatment on the estate in the Tula province.

From his youth Dostoevsky revealed a great attraction to literature, and was a voracious reader. In a letter to his brother Mikhail, on August 9, 1838, for instance, he mentions that besides being penniless, he has kept himself occupied by Goethe's *Faust*, and most of Victor Hugo. (*Pis'ma* 1:45–47.)

Dostoevsky already dreamed of a literary career and thus spent most of his time reading and writing while in the engineering school, waiting out his military commitment which was pressed upon him by his father. In a characteristic mood he wrote to Mikhail, on August 16, 1839: "I am confident in myself. Man is a mystery. It must be solved, and if you spend all your life trying to solve it, you must not say the time has been wasted; I occupy myself with this mystery, for I wish to be a man." (*Pis'ma* 2:550.)

On November 29, 1840, Dostoevsky was promoted to non-commissioned officer's rank; in 1841, to ensign and a year later, lieutenant. But on October 19, 1844, Dostoevsky received his wish and was discharged on account of illness.

Early Career: Success and Failure

From his discharge in October 1844 until April 1849, Dostoevsky published ten novels and short stories. *Poor Folk* (1845), Dostoevsky's first novel, placed the author on the path to the glittering heights of Russian literary society. He was immediately praised and glorified by the foremost literary critics of the day, Vassarion Belinsky, Grigorovitch, and Nekrasov. Nekrasov exuberantly told Belinsky "A new Gogol has appeared!"[11] Belinsky retorted to Nekrasov: "Gogols grow like mushrooms in your midst." (*Diary of a Writer*, 2:586.) But Belinsky overcame his initial scepticism, and demanded: "Bring him here, bring him here as soon as possible!"[12] After reading the work, Belinsky offered his critique. "Honor and glory to the poet whose Muse loves people in garrets and basements and tells the inhabitants of gilded palaces: 'look they are also men, they are also your brethren.'"[13] Indeed, Belinsky hailed Dostoevsky as the successor to Gogol.

Dostoevsky became an instant celebrity at the age of twenty-four. But his star did not long retain its luster; his visions of future triumphs were dashed by the disappointed expectations of his critics. His following efforts, *The Double: A Novel in Nine Letters*, and especially *The Landlady*, and *Prokharchin*, received sharp criticism from Belinsky.

With his fall from the good graces of the literary critics, Dostoevsky suffered another financial crisis, a situation that was never really alleviated until the last years of his life.

Left-wing Involvement: The Petrasheveky Circle

The 1840s were the most unrestrained years of Dostoevsky's life, a period when he underwent a torment of belief and almost lost his faith in Russian Orthodoxy and the link with Jesus Christ. This breakdown of his earlier beliefs reached its apogee during Dostoevsky's short-lived personal relationship with Belinsky and his circle. In late 1845, a group of Belinsky's admirers, so-called Russian Utopian Socialists, began to gather each Friday evening at the home of M. B. Butashevich-Petrasheveky, an official in the Ministry of Foreign Affairs. There they discussed the great questions of the day: the peasant problem, the rigors of censorship, corruption in the government and church, and the progressive ideas of Fourier, Robert Owen, Proudhon, and Saint-Simon.

The Petrasheveky circle was a hotbed of fervent atheists and socialists. Petrashevsky felt, for instance, that "Christ was a well-known demagogue who had ended his career somewhat unsuccessfully."[14] Petrashevsky set up a lending library of banned books for the members to share, including the works of Fourier, Feuerbach, Lamennais, Sismondi, and others. Dostoevsky is recorded as borrowing the works of Louis Blanc, Proudon, Cabet's *Le vrai christianisme suivant Jésus Christ*, and Strauss's *Das Leben Jesu*.

Though the members of the Petrashevsky circle did not share uniform views on political solutions for Russia, they did share a common desire for a new society modeled on Western Europe. A unanimous intense dislike for the autocratic policies of the tsar was a basic tenet of the group. N. Tombelli wrote of Nicholas I: "No, the emperor is not a human being, but a monster, a beast; he is that Antichrist of whom the Apocalypse speaks."[15]

The Durov Circle

Corresponding to the slight divergences in doctrine were more crucial diversities in temperament. Dostoevsky and seven others formed a splinter group, the Durov circle, whose bylaws included the threat of death to anyone who betrayed the cause. The leader of this second group was N. A. Speshnev, a wealthy landowner and ardent atheist and communist.[16]

The period from 1845 to 1849 is especially crucial in Dostoevsky's life. It has evoked much attention, although with divergent interpretations and emphases. For instance, Yarmolinsky is unimpressed by the opinion that Dostoevsky was a militant radical in political and religious matters. In his judgment, "Dostoevsky's views had the quality of continuity which is traditionally denied to him," for "his early radicalism appears more or less apocryphal."[17] In contrast, Simmons stresses the powerful influence that Belinsky and his followers had on Dostoevsky; they "infected Dostoevsky with the dangerous virus of social reform."[18] On Dostoevsky's religion, Simmons says that "there is reason to believe, however, that his faith in the Orthodox Church during this early period was not as solid as is commonly supposed. His close association with the avowed atheist Speshnev, under whose influence and in whose debt he was, is perhaps indicative of the surface character of his religious convictions at the time."[19] Hans Kohn goes so far as to say that "Dostoevsky himself was not a religious man, he never knew the bliss of true religious certainty. Like Ivan Karamazov he was a God-seeker, assailed by all the doubts."[20] A. P. Milyukov denies that the Durov circle was imbued with "revolutionary plans of any kind," and states that the group could not possibly be described as a secret society."[21] Mochulsky questions the radical features of some members of the Durov circle.[22]

In his *Diary* Dostoevsky confessed his attraction to Belinsky and his followers. Belinsky realized, Dostoevsky wrote, that "as a socialist, he had to destroy Christianity in the first place. He knew that the revolution must necessarily begin with atheism." (*Diary* 1:6–7.) "As a socialist, he was duty bound to destroy the teaching of Christ, to call it fallacious and ignorant philanthropy, doomed by modern science and economic tenets." Later he relates a conversation about Christ returning to earth, and Belinsky retorts that, "Precisely, He would join the socialists and follow them." (*Diary*, 8; *see also* 147–51.) Milyukov states that although Dostoevsky read all the works on socialism, he "remained wholly skeptical," seeing the proponents as "honest but foolish, visionaries." (*Letters*, 275.)

The Durov circle commissioned Dostoevsky to set up its printing press and to write articles sympathetic to socialism. Oral readings of banned literature was another offering of the group; at one meeting Dostoevsky presented Belinsky's famous letter to Gogol which assailed Gogol for preaching submission to the Church and State instead of fighting for reform and an entirely new society. Vissarion the Furious's letter was a blistering attack on autocracy, the Orthodox Church, obscurantism, and serfdom. Dostoevsky delivered Belinsky's outraged attack of more than ten pages of text both in the group and in the homes of several friends.

Belinsky and Gogol

Belinsky charged Gogol with not realizing that

> Russia sees her salvation not in mysticism, nor asceticism, nor pietism, but in the successes of civilization, enlightenment and humanity. What she needs is not sermons (she has heard enough of them!) or prayers (she has repeated them too often!), but the awakening in the people of a sense of their human dignity lost for so many centuries amid the dirt and refuse; she needs rights and laws conforming

not with the preaching of the church but with common sense and justice, and their strictest possible observance. . . . Proponent of the knout, apostle of ignorance, champion of obscurantism and Stygian darkness, panegyrist of Tatar morals—what are you about! . . . That you base such teaching on the Orthodox Church I can understand; it has always served as the prop of the knout and the servant of despotism; but why have you mixed Christ up in this? What in common have you found between Him and any church, least of all the Orthodox Church? He was the first to bring to people the teaching of freedom, equality and brotherhood and set the seal of truth to that teaching by martyrdom. . . . Does not the priest in Russia represent for all Russians the embodiment of gluttony, avarice, servility, and shamelessness?. . . Strange! According to you the Russian people is the most religious in the world. That is a lie! The basis of religiousness is pietism, reverence, fear of God. Whereas the Russian man utters the name of the Lord while scratching himself somewhere. He says of the icon: if it isn't good for praying it's good for covering the pots. Take a closer look and you will see that it is by nature a profoundly atheistic people. It still retains a good deal of superstition, but not a trace of religiousness.[23]

Belinsky wrote to Gogol July 15, 1847, from Europe where he had gone for a cure to his illness. In reply, Gogol wrote that "you looked at my book with the eyes of an angry man and therefore took almost everything the wrong way." In a second letter—never sent to Belinsky—after debating numerous points, Gogol admitted "So far I have seen only one thing as an indisputable truth—the fact that I do not know Russia at all, that much has changed since I was there, and that now I have to learn almost everything that is there anew."[24]

Dostoevsky's Arrest

The European upheavals of 1848 and their aftermath brought many anxious moments to Czar Nicholas; thus the members of the Durov and Petrashevsky circles were rounded up and prosecuted. Dostoevsky was arrested on April 23, 1849, and imprisoned in the Petropavlovsk Fortress. The formal government charges included "participation in criminal designs, the circulation of a private letter full of insolent expressions against the Orthodox Church and the Supreme Authority, and an attempt to spread literature against the Government by means of a domestic lithography."[25]

Dostoevsky and fourteen other prisoners were condemned to death. After a mock execution by the firing squad, complete with priest and sermon (recounted by Dostoevsky in *The Idiot*), the group was granted a reprieve "by the infinite clemency of His Majesty the Emperor." The sentences of death were commuted to exile and hard labor. Thus, on Christmas eve, December 24, 1849, Dostoevsky was put in irons and started the long trek from St. Petersburg to Siberia.

Life in Exile: The School of Pain

Dostoevsky spent the next eight years in Eastern Russia, near Omsk for the first four years where he was surrounded by murderers and other criminals. He refers to this period of his life as the "long school." (*Diary*, [1873], 1:9.) There they lived in the bitter isolation and restricting chains, with nausea from poor food and dirty clothes, in stifling summers and severe winters. Dostoevsky writes "we were packed like herrings in a barrel." (*Pis'ma* 1:136.)

For Dostoevsky, one of the most distressing facts of his Siberian exile was that the angry, embittered men refused to accept the "gentlemen" in the camp. "Their hatred for the nobility," he wrote, "is boundless; they regard all of us who belong to it with hostility and emnity. They would have devoured us if they only could." (*Pis'ma* 1:136.) Now the tables were turned. "You nobles have iron beaks, you have torn us to pieces. When you were masters, you torment the people, and now, when times are tough for you, you want to be our brothers." (*Pis'ma* 1:135–36.)

A New Definition of Man

In this environment of stress and hostility, of general uproar filled with "smoke and grime, shaven heads, branded faces, ragged clothes," where everything is "defiled and degraded," Dostoevsky formulated a new definition of man; Man is no longer a mystery. In *The House of the Dead*, he wrote: "What cannot man live through! Man is a creature that can get accustomed to anything, and I think that is the best definition of him." (*The House of the Dead* (New York: Dell, 1965), 34.) "Tyranny is a habit," he writes later, "it may develop, and it does develop at last, into a disease. I maintain that the very best of men may be coarsened and hardened into a brute by habit.

Blood and power intoxicate; coarseness and depravity are developed; the mind and the heart are tolerant of the most abnormal things, till at last they come to relish them." (*House of the Dead*, 240–41.)

Physical and Social Suffering

The prison sentence took its toll on Dostoevsky. According to several naval cadets stationed there, Dostoevsky was dull, awkward, and always taciturn. "On his pale, worn, ashen face, which was freckled with dark-red spots, one never saw a smile." (*Letters*, 283.)[26] Human affability and psychological conditions broke down to such an extent that Durov and Dostoevsky became estranged, seemingly hating one another by not even bothering to exchange one word while in prison. (*Letters*, 286.) Dostoevsky reflects on this prison psychology in a letter to the wife of Decembrist M. A. Fonvizin:

> To be alone is a natural need, like eating and drinking; for in that kind of concentrated communism one becomes a wholehearted enemy of mankind. The constant companionship of others works like poison or plague; and from that unendurable martyrdom I most suffered in the last four years. There were moments in which I hated every men, whether good or evil, and regarded him as a thief who, unpunished, was robbing me of life. The most unbearable part is when one grows unjust, malignant, and evil, is aware of it, even reproves oneself, and yet has not the power to control oneself. (*Letters*, 72.)

Dostoevsky's health was also broken during the Siberian exile. Though there is a difference of opinion about when and where he suffered his first epileptic seizures, probably the first attacks occurred in Omsk, and severe attacks followed in February 1857 after Dostoevsky's marriage.[27]

Dostoevsky himself never had to withstand beatings or corporal punishment in Siberia, albeit the other prisoners underwent that pain at the hands of the guards. In his reminiscences Baron A. Wrangel states that Dostoevsky "told me himself that neither in the prison nor later during the military service was ever a hair of his head hurt by his superiors or by the other prisoners or soldiers; all the newspaper reports that declare otherwise are pure invention." (*Letters*, 290–91.)

Life in Exile: The School of Scripture

Another school which Dostoevsky experienced during his four years in prison near Omsk was the Scriptures. In his *Diary* Dostoevsky refers to the gift of the Bible that the wives of the Decembrists in Tobolsk gave him on his way to Siberia. It was the only book allowed in prison. "It lay for four years under my pillow in penal servitude. Sometimes I read it to myself and sometimes to others. I used it to teach a convict [the Tatar Aley] how to read." (*Diary* 1:9.)[28] Dostoevsky refers to the fact that the Bible was the only book allowed in two of his novels. "A convict who was sincerely attached to me (this is no exaggeration) stole from me a Bible, the only book which one was allowed to have in the prison; he confessed it to me himself the same day, not from repentance, but feeling sorry for me because I spent such a long time looking for it." (*House of the Dead*, 45.) The other involves a scene with Raskolnikov on the last page of *Crime and Punishment*. "Under his pillow lay the New Testament. He took it up mechanically. The book belonged to Sonia; it was the one from which she had read the raising of Lazarus to him." (*Crime and Punishment*, 472.)

Life in Exile: Conversion

Through his countless new experiences, interspersed with his meditations and reflections on the New Testament, Dostoevsky began to rediscover Christ. Scattered references to the Russian attachment to the Orthodox Church also attest to a transformation in Dostoevsky. During the Christmas season the convicts readied themselves for the priest:

> In the middle of the room they put a table, covered it with a clean towel, and on it set the ikon and lighted the lamp before us. At last the priest came with the cross and the holy water. After repeating prayers and singing before the ikon, he stood facing the convicts and all of them with genuine reverence came forward to kiss the cross. Then the priest walked through all the wards and sprinkled them with holy water.... They followed the cross out with the same reverence with which they had welcomed it... (*House of the Dead*, 173.)

Dostoevsky's most touching reference to the convicts' devotion to Orthodoxy concerns the Lenten preparation for Easter, the penetrating experience the liturgy worked on them.

We stood all together in a group close to the church door, so far back that we could only hear the loud-voiced deacon and from time to time catch a glimpse of the black cape and the bald head of the priest through the crowd. . . . we were fettered and branded as felons; everyone avoided us, everyone seemed to be even afraid of is, alms were always given to us, and I remember that this was positively pleasing to me in a way. . . . The convicts prayed very earnestly and every one of them brought his poor farthing to the church every time to buy a candle, or to put in the collection. 'I, too, am a man,' he thought, and felt perhaps as he gave it, in God's eyes we are all equal. . . We took the sacrament at the early mass. When with the chalice in his hands the priest read the words: '. . . accept me, O Lord, even as the thief,' almost all of them bowed down to the ground with a clanking of chains, apparently applying the words literally to themselves. (*House of the Dead*, 272–73.)

Dostoevsky's "Creed"

On February 15, 1854, Dostoevsky ended his term at Omsk and was sent as a soldier to a battalion in Semipalatinsk, an Asiatic hellhole. In early March he wrote to Mrs. N. D. Fonvizin, his contact with the outside world during his stay in prison, and expressed his problems of unbelief.

I want to say to you, about myself, that I am a child of this age, a child of unbelief and skepticism, and probably (indeed I know it) shall remain so to the end of my life. How dreadfully has it tormented me (and torments me even now)—this longing for faith, which is all the stronger for the proofs I have against it. And yet God gives me sometimes moments of perfect peace; in such moments I love and believe that I am loved; in such moments I have formulated my creed, wherein all is clear and holy to me. This creed is extremely simple; here it is: I believe that there is nothing lovelier, deeper, more sympathetic, more rational, more manly, and more perfect than the Savior; I say to myself with jealous love that not only is there no one else like Him, but that there could be no one. I would even say more: If anyone could prove to me that Christ is outside the truth, and if the truth *really did* exclude Christ, I should prefer to stay with Christ and not with truth. (*Letters*, 70–71.)

Mochulsky comments on Dostoevsky's recovery or description of his faith.

Dostoevsky's 'symbol of faith' was far from the symbol of Nicea, and his religious thought still bore little resemblance to the faith of the Orthodox Church. He opposed to Belinsky's atheistic rationalism Christian humanism, not faith in the God-man Christ, but love for *Christ the man.* For him Christ was only the most beautiful 'sympathetic,' and perfect of men. He even allowed that the One who said of Himself: 'I am the Truth,' can be found to exist outside the truth; this premise is blasphemous to every believer. Here is the direction in which Dostoevsky's convictions were regenerated.[29]

Mochulsky recapitulates his argument: "This fully corroborates our designating Dostoevsky's religiosity as *Christian humanism.* His rapturous love for the human image of Christ was still far from ecclesiastical Orthodoxy."[30]

Mochulsky's interpretation may seem severe at first glance, for Dostoevsky was fond of making extreme statements to prove a point or stir up controversy, but Baron Alexander Wrangel's account of his conversations and friendship with Dostoevsky bear this out: "We seldom spoke of religion. He was at heart religious, though he rarely entered a church; the popes (priests) and especially the Siberian ones, he could not stand at all. Of Christ he would speak with moving rapture." (*Letters*, 304.)

Shift in Dostoevsky's Themes

There is no denying that Dostoevsky's four-year-long school played a crucial role in his development as a thinker and writer. His personal letters and his novel on prison life, *The House of the Dead*, provide ample evidence of this influence. Indeed, the best testimony to his inner transformation is the new range of themes of Dostoevsky's writings. He shifts his emphasis from sociological to psychological, ethical, moral, and religious problems. Faith and salvation through human suffering in the person of Raskolnikov marks the first radical turn in Dostoevsky's new creative concerns, underlining, in a way, his own "passport back to Russia."

Unbelief and Atheism

The story of Raskolnikov includes an interesting passage on the problem of faith and unbelief.

The second week in Lent, his turn came to take the sacrament with his gang. He went to church and prayed with the others. A quarrel broke out one day, he did not know how. All fell on him at once in a fury. 'You're an infidel! You don't believe in God,' they shouted. 'You ought to be killed.' He had never talked to them about God nor his belief, but they wanted to kill him as an infidel. He said nothing. One of the prisoners rushed at him in a perfect frenzy. Raskolnikov awaited him calmly and silently; his eyebrows did not quiver, his face did not flinch. The guard succeeded in intervening between him and his assailant, or there would have been bloodshed."
(*Crime and Punishment*, 468.)

Is this scene based on an experience of Dostoevsky himself?[31]

Atheism was of course the most heinous crime imaginable. However weak Dostoevsky's link with Christ may have been previously, he was certainly no atheist. In this regard, Simmons offers the standard interpretation of the change brought about in Dostoevsky over his four-year prison sentence:

In truth, the experiences of these four years as a convict played an important part, perhaps the most important part, in Dostoevsky's entire development. He entered the prison a young radical, and he left it with a heightened respect for the authority of the crown and for the established order of things. He entered it something of an agnostic and left prison with a firmer faith in the teaching of Christ and a stronger belief in the saving grace of the Orthodox Church in the troubled existence of Russia.[32]

Yarmolinsky, for one, does not share the particular interpretation, holding for the notion of greater continuity between Dostoevsky's youth and mature years.

Dostoevsky was especially enthusiastic about the new czar, Alexander II. In a letter to Wrangel, April 12, 1956, he comments: "You write that everybody loves the new Tsar. I myself idolize him." (*Letters*, 97.)

Regaining some of his lost freedom, Dostoevsky immediately wrote to his brother, asking for a host of books to make up for his four-year intellectual vacuum while in prison. These included the works of Guizot, Hegel, Kant, Thierry, Thiers, Ranke, the Koran as well as the Fathers of the Church and church histories. In retrospect, he writes: "Decidedly I have not spent my time there in vain. I have learned to know the Russian people as only a few know them. I am a little vain of it. I hope that such vanity is pardonable." (*Letters*, 97.)

Later Dostoevsky writes to General E. I. Todleben for permission to write and publish once more. The chastened writer reflects with the general on his "change of heart" effected by the Siberian experience.

> I was guilty, and am very conscious of it. I was convicted of the intention (but only the intention) of acting against the Government; I was lawfully and quite justly condemned; the hard and painful experiences of the ensuing years have sobered me, and altered my views in many respects. But then, while I was still blind, I believed in all the theories and Utopias.... I had not one single being within reach with whom I could exchange a cordial word; I endured hunger, cold, sicknesses; I suffered from the hard labors and the hatred of my companions the criminals, who bore me a grudge for being an officer and a well-born person. And yet I swear to you that none of those torments was greater than that which I felt when I realized my errors, and saw in banishment I was cut off from my fellow creatures and unable to serve them with all my powers, desires and capacities...
> [It is grievous] to feel that I have the power and the talent to do something which would really atone for the worthlessness of my earlier activities, and yet to languish in impotence. (*Letter*, 91 ff.)

Marriage

On February 6, 1857, Dostoevsky married the widow Maria Dmtryevna Issayev. Two months later the title of nobility was restored to him and his legal heirs. In July 1859, thanks to the assistance of Baron Wrangel and other friends, Dostoevsky was able to leave Semipalatinsk and reside in Tver. Toward the end of November of that years his petition to return to Moscow and St. Petersburg was finally granted.

Renewal of Career

Dostoevsky returned to Russia from his ten-year exile with renewed hopes that the liberal atmosphere of Alexander II would allow him to begin anew with a flourish. One of his first major ventures was to collaborate with his brother, Mikhail, Apollon Grigoryev, and Nikolay Strakhov on a new periodical, *Vremya* (Time).

Reconciliation of Westernizers and Slavophiles

One goal of this new project was to attempt to reconcile the Westerners and the Slavophiles. The prospectus of the journal read in part:

> We have at last persuaded ourselves that we too are a separate nationality, independent and original in the highest degree, and that our task is to create for ourselves an indigenous form native to *our own soil*. . . . We foresee that. . . the Russian idea may well be a synthesis of all the ideas that have developed in Europe.[33]

The group centered around *Vremya* referred to themselves as the *pochvenniki* or men rooted in the soil of the motherland. All problems, therefore, would be properly solved within the native environment based on the energy, ingenuity, and resourcefulness of the Russian peasant masses.

The sixties meant another decade of unrest and searching for Dostoevsky. After adapting to the new situation in Russia, he decided to fulfill and old childhood wish of traveling to Europe. There he spend two and a half months, stopping off at the major cities including London, where he visited the self-imposed exile, Alexander Herzen, who found the young writer "naive, somewhat muddled, but very nice," and professing an "enthusiastic belief in the Russian people." (*Winter Notes*, 30)

Vremya *Suppressed*

In May 1863 the Russian government suppressed *Vremya* because it objected to an article by Strakhov on the Polish question. Borrowing funds, Dostoevsky made his second trip abroad from August to October 1863. On March 24, 1864, Dostoevsky launched a new journal, *Epokha* [*Epoch*], to replace *Vremya*.

Notes from the Underground: *A New Definition of Man*

In the same year he published *Notes from the Underground*, in which he revised the definition of man. Man is neither a mystery, nor a person who can get used to anything, but a *volitional* animal. "You see, gentlemen, reason is an excellent thing, there's no disputing that, but reason is nothing but reason and satisfies only the rational side of man's nature, while will is a manifestation of the whole life, that is, of the whole human life including reason and all the impulses." (*Notes from the Underground*, 48.) "Confronted by "self-evident truths, he [Dostoevsky], insults them, mocks them, sticks out his tongue at them. He wishes to live not according to rational freedom but according to his own 'foolish' freedom."[34]

Deaths in the Family

In the spring of 1864 Dostoevsky faced a double setback. On April 16 his wife died after a long bout with consumption. The marriage had been unhappy, and undoubtedly the feelings of remorse were mixed with a sense of relief. Then on June 10 his brother Mikhail died, and he prematurely volunteered to assume the support of his brother's family and other relatives. Burdened with debts, Dostoevsky fled to Europe for the third time in late July 1865.

Dostoevsky returned to Russia in November 1865, ready to publish his new novel, *Crime and Punishment*. Here again, the author was engrossed with the notion of the volitional animal, in what would ironically become the archetype of Nietzsche's Superman, the heretic Raskolnikov.

Remarriage

On February 15, 1867, Dostoevsky married his stenographer, Anna G. Snitkin, and left for Europe on April 14th, Dostoevsky's fourth trip abroad. They did not return until four years later, in June of 1871. Once again he had to readjust to the changing conditions of his homeland. Once more he had to seek connections with the leading literary, intellectual, and political circles. In a burst of literary activity, Dostoevsky published *The Idiot, The Devils, The Diary of a Writer, A Raw Youth*, and *The Brothers Karamazov*, an amazing feat for the space of ten years.

Dostoevsky reached the pinnacle of his fame on June 8, 1880, when he delivered his famous address on Pushkin at the meeting of

the Society of Lovers of Russian Literature. All his wishes were fulfilled. As he mentions in a letter to his wife a little more than a week
before the event, "If my speech at the ceremony is successful, then
henceforth I shall be more famous as a writer in Moscow and therefore throughout Russia. I mean famous in the sense of greatness such
as Turgenev and Tolstoy have already won for themselves." (*Letters
to His Wife*, 305.)

Deepening of Dostoevsky's Themes

The torrents of literature that Dostoevsky turned out in the seventies
represented a steady progression in his thought pattern. His pre-
exilic period reflected an acute social consciousness. Then following
his return from Siberia, he began to explore the implications of the
problem of good and evil, the problem of ethics in mass society. After
his return from Europe, Dostoevsky reached a more subtle plateau
in applying ideological and religious thought to the conditions of his
homeland and the rest of the world.

The major premise underlying all of Dostoevsky's work, despite
his avowed passionate advocacy of freedom and his description of the
volatile and vulnerable nature of the human will, is that—try as man
may—the kingdom of God is not attainable here on earth. "My kingdom is not of this world. If my kingdom were of this world, my followers would have fought that I might not be delivered to the Jews.
But, as it is, my kingdom is not from here" (John 18:36). Instead,
there is an overabundance of suffering.

> [Dostoevsky] was not a believer in progress, and he condemned
> modern civilization as being materialistic and mechanistic. The end
> of history was not the creation of an earthly paradise, a vain and dan-
> gerous utopia, but the advent of the eternal city of God. In anticipa-
> tion of that apocalyptic event, man's duty here on earth was to strive
> for then unity in Christ with his fellowmen. All attempts to unify
> humanity on any other basis, by means of outward authority, by so-
> cial and political reforms alone, or by appealing to utilitarian argu-
> ments, were bound to end in a tragic failure.[35]

The compelling figure in Dostoevsky's personal and creative life
was, of course, Jesus Christ. In a letter to S. A. Ivanova from Geneva
in January 1868, Dostoevsky confesses his admiration for the person
of Christ: "There is only one positively beautiful person in the

world—Christ, so that the appearance of this boundlessly, infinitely beautiful person is of course an infinite miracle in itself (the entire Gospel of St. John is written in this sense; he finds the whole miracle in the incarnation alone, the manifestation of the beautiful)."[36]

Dostoevsky's wife described the moving impression that the Holbein picture of Christ taken from the cross made on him while they were in Basel in 1867. In *The Idiot* there is a picture of this painting in Rogozhin's house; Myshkin exemplifies Dostoevsky's own experience: "I saw the picture abroad and I can't forget it." (*The Idiot*, 212.)

The Central Theme of the Christ

Dostoevsky slowly began to conceive the plan of manifesting this truly beautiful person to the world, to pull down from heaven the figure of Christ and to portray Him in a flesh and blood human. In a letter to A. N. Maikov on January 12, 1868, he discusses the early stages of his proposed novel. "For a long time now a certain idea has been bothering me, but I have been afraid to write a novel out of it because the idea is much too difficult and I am not prepared for it, though the idea is quite enticing and I love it. The idea—is to portray the completely beautiful person. There is nothing more difficult to do than this, especially in our own times." (*Pis'ma*, 2:61.)

In a second letter to Maikov, on April 8, 1870, Dostoevsky again mentioned that he was thinking about a gigantic novel to consist of five parts with the general title of "The Life of a Great Sinner." The novel would center around a question "with which I have been tormented, consciously or unconsciously all my life—that is, the existence of God." (*Pis'ma*, 2:264.) Here again Dostoevsky is taken up with the "positively holy figure," the "Russian positive type which our literature is seeking, and not a Lavrovsky, Chichikov, Rahmetov or others, nor Lopuhova or Rahmetovs. True, I will not create anything new, I will only represent the real Tikhon, whom I have for so long accepted into my heart with delight." (*Pis'ma*, 2:264.)

Dostoevsky's first major attempt to portray the positively beautiful man began with the figure of Myshkin (Prince Christ) in *The Idiot*. With Myshkin, the meek or mouse-like individual, Dostoevsky launched into a new phase of his creative life. He was not merely attempting to depict the thoroughly "good man"; there was much more to the venture. Dostoevsky sought to cast Myshkin in the role of a shaper, a reconciler, a rehabilitator of society, in a word, what he hoped would be the real "Orthodox man."

Orthodoxy as Integrating Factor in Russian Life

For Dostoevsky, Orthodoxy was *the* integrating factor in Russian life; it alone could reconstruct the lost image of Christ in the world. At first this notion and conviction was advanced cautiously and almost imperceptibly in kernel form, but from the creation of Myshkin and his works of the seventies, the *Diary* in particular, the force of this argument is developed with greater strength and intensity.

According to Dostoevsky, Orthodoxy formed the foundation of Russian life. (*Diary*, [April 1876], 1:287.) This was a self-evident truth, inherent in the Russian consciousness since it first embraced Christianity.

> And she had tacitly comprehended that she bore within herself a treasure which was no longer in existence anywhere else— Orthodoxy; that she was the conservatrix of Christ's truth, genuine truth—the true image of Christ which had been dimmed in all other religions and in all other nations. This treasure, this eternal truth inherent in Russia and of which she had become the custodian, according to the view of the best Russians of those days, as it were, relieved their conscience of the duty of any other enlightenment. (*Diary*, [June 1876], 1:360.)

Orthodoxy, according to Dostoevsky, encompasses everything that man could ask for.

> Isn't there in Orthodoxy alone both the truth and salvation of the Russian people, and—in the forthcoming centuries—of mankind as a whole? Hasn't there been preserved in Orthodoxy alone, in all its purity the Divine image of Christ? And, perhaps, the most momentous preordained destiny of the Russian people, within the destinies of mankind at large, consists in the preservation in their midst of the Divine image of Christ, in all its purity, and, when the time comes, in the revelation of this image to the world which has lost its way! (*Diary*, [June 1873], 1:63.)

The *Diary*, as an open-ended vehicle for the widest possible expression of views, naturally lent itself to the repetition of his ideas and formulations. He later said, "The lost image of Christ in all the light of its purity is conserved in Orthodoxy." (*Diary*, 2:906.)

After authenticating Orthodoxy for preserving the treasures of Christianity intact, Dostoevsky links Orthodoxy with the Russian people. In his view, they are inseparable. "Russian religion, Russian Orthodoxy, is everything the Russian people regard as their sanctity: in it are their ideals, the whole truth and rectitude of life. And what united and what kept the Slavic nations alive in the days of their distress, during the four centuries of the Mohammedan yoke—what but their religion?" (*Diary*, [September, 1875], 1:438.) Thus "the whole destiny of Russia lies in Orthodoxy," because it is "the light from the East," because "Orthodoxy is everything." (*Pis'ma*, 2:292; *Biography*, 360.)

Since Russia and Orthodoxy are so closely related, even identified, Dostoevsky makes it clear that one cannot be understood without the other. Anything less is mere pretension. "He who does not understand Orthodoxy—that same person will never understand anything of the people." (Biography, 360.) Riasanovsky, in his classical treatment of the topic, comments on the general trend of the slavophile doctrine.

> Russia could not be separated from Orthodox Christianity, and it was useless to study the history of the Russian people apart from Orthodoxy. This religious element was of an absolute higher order than any national or racial traits, and it provided the content and the gauge of Russia, Russian culture, and the Russians. . . . The Russian people was the only truly Christian people on earth; according to Konstantin Aksakov, Russian history could be read as one of the lives of the saints. Russia could not stop short of the Christian ideal: 'Nothing can be done about it, Russia must either be the most moral, that is the most Christian, of all human societies, or nothing; but it is easier for her not to be than to be nothing.'[37]

At first, especially when *Vremya* and *Epokha* became realities, Dostoevsky declared himself in the middle of the road; he would reconcile the Westerners and the Slavophiles. But it is perfectly clear which position he would favor in the years to come, particularly in the late sixties and seventies. His ideas resemble Gogol's belief that Orthodoxy had the "potentiality of solving all the problems which have now been posed so sharply before all mankind," for it "has the power to resolve all our perplexities, quandaries, and problems."[38]

An even closer parallel is seen in a Gogol's letter of March 30, 1849 to A. M. Vielgorgskaya:

> The high merit of the Russian race consists in the fact that more than others it is capable of taking into itself the elevated word of the Gospels which leads to the perfection of men. The seeds of the heavenly sower were scattered everywhere with equal generosity. But some fell close to the public road and were all devoured by birds which swooped down; others fell on stone, germinated, but dried up; a third kind fell among the thorns—they germinated but were quickly smothered by harmful weeds; only the fourth kind which fell on good earth brought forth fruit. This good earth is the receptive Russian nature. Christ's seeds, well-cherished in the heart, gave all that is best in the Russian character. Therefore, in order to become Russian it is necessary to turn to the source, to have recourse to the means without which a Russian will not become Russian in the higher meaning of this word. Perhaps only the Russian is destined to feel the meaning of life more closely.[39]

The Slavophiles received their impetus and inspiration from K. S. Aksakov (1817–60), Alexis S. Khomyakov (1804–60), and Ivan V. Kireevski (1806–56). The movement flourished from 1840 to 1860. The group idealized the concept of the Russian peasant commune in their struggle against individualism. According to Khomyakov, "The truth is inaccessible to individual thinkers. It is accessible only to the aggregate of thinkers *bound together by love.*"[40] Conciliar consciousness or *sobornost*, which stressed unity in freedom was the keynote of the slavophile movement.[41]

Love for the Masses

Dostoevsky's avowed admiration and love for the unlettered masses leaps from the pages of the *Diary*. Yet he was aware of the gulf that separated these "holy," though highly superstitious, people from the often skeptical, agnostic, or atheistic strata of Russian intellectual society. Dostoevsky absorbed the populist spirit, striving mightily to find means of reconciling these two unequal classes of society. The future of Russia depended on this reconciliation; to realize this goal, the intellectuals must generally accept the fact that true wisdom was found in the masses.

In the present and future destinies of Orthodox Christianity lies the whole idea of the Russian people; therein is their service to Christ and their thirst for the exploit on Christ's behalf. This is a genuine thirst—a great and unceasing thirst—which has been burning in our people since the most ancient times, and this is an extremely important fact as it characterizes our people and our state. (*Diary*, [December 1876], 1:555.)

That Dostoevsky was keenly aware of a contrary opinion is evident. "Because I preach faith in God and in the people, the gentry would like to see me disappear from the face of the earth." (*Letters*, 259.) "About the faith of the people and about Orthodoxy we possess merely a couple of dozens of liberal and obscene anecdotes, and we delight in scoffing stories about how an old woman confesses her sins to the priest and how a peasant prays to Friday." (*Diary*, [April 1976], 1:286.) "'Even though this mass always called itself Christian, nevertheless, it has no conception of either religion or even Christ; it knows not even the most ordinary prayers.' This is what is usually being said about our people." (*Diary*, [March 1877], 2:630.) Evidently, Dostoevsky was aware of the great difficulties of his task. Yet he was insistent. He must make his case logical or at least plausible to the thinkers and his audience. The stumbling block was the lack of education for the Russian masses. Thus he retorts:

I assert that our people have long been enlightened, having embraced in their hearts Christ and his teachings. It may be argued that the people do not know the teachings of Christ, and that no sermons are being preached to them. But this is a vain objection: they know everything, precisely that they have to know, although they could not pass an examination in catechism. The people acquired their knowledge in churches where, for centuries, they have been listening to prayers and hymns which are better than sermons. They have been repeating and singing these prayers in forests, fleeing from their enemies, as far back as the time of Batyi's invasion; they have been singing: *Almighty Lord, be with us!* It may have been then that they memorized this hymn because at that time nothing but Christ was left to them; yet in this hymn alone is Christ's whole truth. And what is there in the fact that few sermons are preached to the people and that chanters are muttering unintelligibly? . . . As against this, the priest reads: 'God and Lord of my being,' etc.—and in this prayer *the whole essence of Christianity* is contained, its entire catechism, and the people know this prayer by heart. Likewise, they know by heart the life-histories of many a saint; they relate them and listen to them with emotion. (*Diary*, [August 1880], 2:983.)

Dostoevsky briefly explains how the unlettered peasant could possibly love Christ better than other levels of society, facing the old axiom of what you don't know, you don't love. In Dostoevsky's view the Russian people have been carrying Christ

in their hearts from time immemorial. Of this there can be no doubt. How is the true conception of Christ possible without religious teaching?—This is a different question. But the heart-knowledge of Christ, a true conception of Him, does fully exist. It is being passed from generation to generation, and it has merged with the heart of the people. Perhaps, Christ is the only love of the Russian people, and they love His image in their own way, to the limits of sufferance. And, more than on anything else, the people pride themselves on the name 'orthodox,' that is, as confessing Christ more genuinely than all others. I repeat, much may be known unconsciously. (*Diary*, [1873], 1:38–39.)

When Dostoevsky's arguments did not convince his readers, the author referred to a predominant theme of all of his mature works, from *The Idiot* to *The Brothers Karamazov*: the notion of redemption through human suffering. Man experiences, learns, grows, and saves himself in suffering in this world. As he says, "the principal school of Christianity from which they have graduated is—those centuries of innumerable and interminable sufferings which they have endured in the course of their history, when, forsaken and oppressed by everybody, toiling for everybody, they remained with no one but Christ—the Consoler Whom they then embraced forever in their soul, and Who, as, a reward for this, has saved their soul from despair!" (*Diary*, [August 1880], 2:983.)

Cherniavsky comments on this notion. "In their suffering, however, the Russian people had Christ alone as a consoler. More than that, in effect Dostoevsky argued that it was only through suffering that they received Christ, that anyone can receive Christ. Hence the suffering of the Russian people was, in fact, proof that they had Christ in them."[42]

Dostoevsky never gave up his belief in the masses and their inherent devotion to Orthodoxy. Almost to his last days, he affirmed this position time after time. In one final burst of enthusiasm for his last number of the *Diary*, he identified the masses with Orthodoxy.

> Here I shall repeat my own words which I uttered long ago: The overwhelming mass of the Russian people is Orthodox; it lives by the idea of Orthodoxy in all its completeness despite the fact that rationally and scientifically they do not comprehend this idea. *Essentially*, save for this 'idea' there dwells no other in our people; everything is derived from it—at least this is what the people want wholeheartedly and with deep conviction. They want precisely everything they possess and everything that is given them, to emanate exclusively from this idea. (*Diary*, [January 1881], 2:1028.)

Now that Dostoevsky's exuberant faith in both Orthodoxy and the Russian masses is firmly established, the groundwork is laid for one of the most provocative ideas to come from nineteenth century Russian literary and philosophical circles. As early as March 30, 1869, in a letter to Nikolai Strakhov, Dostoevsky makes reference to a "Russian Christ":

> I am not quite sure that Danilevsky will dwell *with sufficient* emphasis upon what is the inmost essence, and the ultimate destiny of the Russian nation; namely, that Russia must reveal to the world her own Russian Christ, whom as yet the peoples know not, and who is rooted in our native Orthodox faith. *There* lies, as I believe, the inmost essence of our vast impending contribution to civilization, whereby we shall awaken the European peoples; there lies the inmost core of our exuberant and intense existence that is to be. (*Letters*, 175.)

Vocation of Russia

Dostoevsky derived this new concept and reality from his peculiar experience and interpretation of the religious spectrum from the extreme of Russian atheism to the "Russian Christ." At one end atheism was the most deadly offense from which all other evils sprang. In a letter to Dr. A. F. Blagonravov on December 19, 1880, he wrote:

> You judge quite rightly that I consider all evil to be grounded in unbelief, and maintain that he who negates nationalism, by the same token, denies his faith as well. This applies especially to Russia, for with us national consciousness is based on Christianity. The words

peasant and Orthodox Russia—these are our basic roots. A Russian who rejects nationality (and there are many who do) is certainly either an atheist or indifferent to religious questions. And the converse: an atheist or indifferent individual cannot possibly understand the Russian people and Russian nationalism. (*Pis'ma*, 4:220.)

Dostoevsky had taken this position as far back as October 21, 1870, in a letter to Maikov: "Observe this my dear friend: He who loses his people and nationality, that person loses his father's faith and belief in God. And if you would like to know—that is the theme of my novel [*The Devils*]." (*Pis'ma*, 2:291.) The same idea is brought forth in the *Diary* for 1873 "Having detached themselves from the people, they naturally also lost God. The restless among them became atheists; the apathetic and placid ones waxed indifferent." (*Diary*, 1:5.)

The basis for this development in Dostoevsky's thought springs from the early sixties and the formation of the *pochvenniki*, men who were rooted it the Russian soil.

They taught that only from the Russian soil, and from the Russian peasant masses attached to the soil, could the Russian intellectual draw life-giving forces. If he uproots himself, he loses his substance and becomes a mere parody of himself. Twenty years later, in his famous speech on Pushkin, Dostoevsky was to return to his attack upon the uprooted intellectual who strays away from soil and people and a *skitalets*, a homeless wanderer, seeks for alien traditions and sources.[43]

Dostoevsky saved the most dramatic exposition of his "Russian Christ," as mentioned in the letter to Maikov, for his novel *The Devils*. There Shatov says that "if an uprising were started in Russia, it would have to begin with atheism." (*The Possessed*, 214.) Furthermore, "A Russian can't be godless," for "as soon as he becomes godless, he ceases to be Russian." (*The Possessed*, 235.) Shatov expresses what he believes to be the indispensable need of belief in God and his own people for rational living: "And a man who has no country has no God either. Rest assured that those who cease to understand the people of their own country and lose contact with them also lose the faith of their forefathers and become godless or indifferent. Yes, yes, it always proves true; that's why you and the lot of us today are either despicable atheists or indifferent, vicious human muck. (*The Possessed*, 40.)

Shatov goes so far as to say that man cannot even make the right choice of good and evil in life without belief in God and country. "You've lost the ability to destinguish good and evil because you've lost touch with the people of your country." (*The Possessed*, 242.) Even more strikingly, Shatov reminds Nikolai Stavrogin of an earlier statement, "One who is not Russian Orthodox cannot be a Russian." (*The Possessed*, 235.)

The Most Sublime Theme

The problem of atheism and belief in God is a constantly recurring theme in Dostoevsky's later works. In the *Diary* for December 1876, he addressed this difficulty:

> Neither man nor nation can exist without a sublime idea. And on earth there is *but one* sublime idea—namely, the idea of the immortality of man's soul—since all other 'sublime' ideas of life, which give life to man, *are merely derived from this one idea.* . . . I assert (again, as yet, without producing any proof) that love of mankind is unthinkable, unintelligible and *altogether impossible without the accompanying faith in the immortality of man's soul.* Those who, having deprived man of the faith in his immortality, are seeking to substitute for it—as life's loftiest aim—'love of mankind,' those, I maintain, are lifting their arm against themselves, since in lieu of love of mankind they are planting in the heart of him who has lost his faith seeds of hatred of mankind." (*Diary*, 1:540–41.)

Dostoevsky even has thirteen-year-old Kolya in *The Brother Karamazov* mouth some of the traditional positions of unbelievers, for instant, that if there were no God he would have to be invented. He also asks if it is possible for a nonbeliever to love mankind, a point that Dostoevsky is making here. Kolya remarks: "Come, you want obedience and mysticism. You must admit that the Christian religion, for instance, has only been of use to the rich and powerful to keep the lower classes in slavery, that's so, isn't it? . . . I am not opposed to Christ, if you like. He was a most humane person, and if He were alive today, He would be found in the ranks of the revolutionists, and would perhaps play a conspicuous part. (*Brothers Karamazov*, 671–72.) The last remark is an obvious echo of the Belinsky circle.[44]

Shatov opens the way for the positive and phenomenal mission of Russia. He asks Stavrogin the surprising question: "Do you know which is the one and only God-bearing nation on earth, destined to regenerate and save the world in the name of the new God—the nation that alone holds the keys of life and the New Word? Do you know what the name of that nation is?" (*The Possessed*, 234.) Shatov gives his own answer by saying that there is only one God-bearing nation, and that is Russia. When Stavrogin question the basis of logic of such an affirmation, indicating that God is being reduced to a simple attribute of nationality, Shatov replies, "It's the other way around; I'm raising the nation to God. And indeed, has it ever been otherwise? A people forms the body of its god." (*The Possessed*, 238.) Shatov explains his position in greater detail, tying all the links together in his profession of the Russian Christ:

> The objective of any nationalist movement in any people at any time is actually a search for God, for their own national God—and it must, above all, be their own God—and belief in Him as the only true God. God's personality is a synthesis of the entire nation from the beginning of its existence to its end. Never have all nations—or even many of them—shared one common God; each of them has always had its own God. When gods become common, it is a sign that nations are doomed to disappear. When gods are shared, they die; and belief in them dies as the nations disappear. The more vital a people, the more individual and special its God. (*The Possessed*, 237.)

Since Orthodoxy had preserved the pristine message of Christ and since Orthodoxy is identified with the Russian thirst for exploit on Christ's behalf—to us his own words—and because the Russian people are the "God-bearing" nation, Dostoevsky believed that a new age was dawning in Russia. A transformation of Russian society would eventually filter into the entire world. But before this new era could be set into motion, the intellectual skeptics of the day had to reconcile themselves with the large mass of unsophisticated Russians. In a letter to Dr. Blagonravov from St. Petersburg on December 19, 1880, Dostoevsky forecasts this new era: "But a new generation is on the way, which will desire union with the people. The first sign of true fellowship with the people is veneration and love for that which the great mass of the people loves and venerates—that is to say, for its God and its faith." (*Letters*, 258.)

If the different levels of Russian society could be reconciled, the transformation of the entire world would follow naturally. Dostoevsky expresses the same idea in a letter to Maikov from

Geneva on March 1, 1868: "The whole world is being prepared for a great renewal by means of Russian thought (which, you are quite right, is compactly welded with Orthodoxy) and this will be achieved within a century perhaps—this is my passionate belief." (*Pis'ma*, 2:81.)

The New Word

According to Dostoevsky, Moscow was ordered to lead the process of transforming the world. The city of the "Great Russians" was destined to utter a "new word." "In my judgment, Moscow—this center of the Great Russians—is designed to live long, and let's pray God that it be so. Moscow, thus far, has not been the third Rome; and the prophecy that 'there shall be no fourth Rome' must be fulfilled. Nor can the world do without a Rome." (*Diary*, [May 1876], 1:315.)

In the following issue of the *Diary*, Dostoevsky spelled out in greater detail what he meant by Orthodox Russia's gift of the new word to the world. He referred to a special union and reconciliation of peoples and nations through the brotherhood of man, a "union founded upon the principles of common service to mankind, and, finally, in man's regeneration based on the true principles of Christ. And if the belief in this "new word" which may be uttered by Russia, heading united Orthodoxy, is a "Utopia" worthy of nothing but ridicule, let people class me, too, among these Utopians, while the ridicule—leave that to me." (*Diary* [June 1876], 1:365.)

In the issue of the *Diary* for January of the following year, Dostoevsky identified himself with the slavophile view of Russia's mission in the world:

> In direct, clear and precise statements they have been asserting that Russia, in conjunction with Slavdom, and at its head, will utter to the whole world the greatest word ever heard, and that that word will precisely be a covenant of universal human fellowship, and no longer in the spirit of personal egoism by means of which at present men and nations unnaturally, because of the struggle for existence, unite with each other in their civilization, setting moral boundaries to the free spirit by positive science, at the same time digging ditches for each other and spreading about each other lies, blasphemy and calumnies. (*Diary* [February 1877], 2:578.)

Dostoevsky suggested that Russia alone has the authentic inner drive and thirst for universal union. This had been her heritage and her special prerogative. Simply by becoming more aware of her strength and destiny, she will be able to complete this mission:

> We should then become convinced that the genuine social truth resides in no one else but our people; that their idea, their spirit contains the living urge of universal communion of men, a fellowship with full respect for national individualities, for their preservation, for the maintenance of complete liberty of men, with the indication of what liberty comprises, i.e., loving communion, guaranteed by deed, by the living example, by the factual need of brotherhood, and not under the threat of the guillotine, not by means of chopping off millions of heads. (*Diary* [January 1877], 2:582.)

Dostoevsky saved his most dramatic expression of what Russia's new word to the world entailed for his triumphant reception during his address on Pushkin. There he recapitulated, within the allotted time, his most cherished reflections and inspiration gathered over the years spent on the *Diary* and on his major novels. At this time he indicated what it meant in his view to be a real Russian: in a word, one who seeks to reconcile all controversies. Such Russians can thereby pave the way for world harmony based on the brotherly accord of all nations abiding by the law of Christ's gospel.

Russia was eminently qualified to fulfill her historical mission because she underwent the necessary preparatory stage. Russia had suffered much and thereby was assured of the power and resources for the task. Though doomed to silence for so many centuries, the Russian people were ready to relay their blessings to the rest of the world. The Russian people, he wrote, "have always possessed great powers for clarifying and settling many bitter and fatal misunderstandings of the Western European civilization." The closing lines of his Pushkin address recapitulated this idea; he commented on Russia's coming to grips with her own special destiny. "I am speaking merely of the brotherhood of man and of the fact that the Russian heart is more adapted to universal, all-humanitarian brotherly fellowship than any other nation. I perceive this is our history, in our gifted men, in the creative genius of Pushkin. (*Diary*, [August 1880], 2:980.)

Dostoevsky saw Russia's special destiny as a servant in the world community. His country's contribution would be a love of service.

As early as June 1875, he writes along these lines in his *Diary*. There he speaks of the longing to his people "to be just and to seek nothing but truth. Briefly, this is, perhaps, the beginning of that active application of our treasure—of Orthodoxy—to the universal service of mankind to which Orthodoxy is designated and which, in fact, constitutes its essence." (*Diary*, [June 1876], 1:361.)

Russia's role as servant to mankind evolved, Dostoevsky believed, in the years following the Petrine reform. In his view Russia sacrificed her own goals and national fulfillment for the betterment of Europe. In his Pushkin speech he raised this point as a truth of history. "For what else has Russia been doing in her policies, during these two centuries, then serving Europe much more than herself? I do not believe that this took place because of the mere want of aptitude on the part of our statesmen." (*Diary*, [August 1880], 2:979.) Dostoevsky makes the same point more forcefully when he has Versilov declare that "only Russia lives not for herself, but for an idea, and, you must admit, my dear, the remarkable fact that for almost the last hundred years Russian has lived absolutely not for herself but for the other States of Europe!" (*A Raw Youth*, 465.)

Dostoevsky viewed Russia's specific task of service to the world as spearheading unity, bringing nations and peoples together. Under this concept he championed the notion of the "all around man." Referring to the after effects of the Petrine reform he wrote:

> Indeed, at once we began to strive impetuously for the most vital universal all-humanitarian fellowship. Not inimically (as it would seem it should have happened) but in a friendly manner, with full love, we admitted into our soul the genius of foreign nations, without any racial discrimination, instinctively managing—almost from the first step—to eliminate contradictions, to excuse and reconcile differences, thereby manifesting our readiness and proclivity to enter into an all-embracing, universal communion with all the nationalities of the great Aryan races.
>
> Yes, the Russian's destiny is incontestably all-European and universal. To become a genuine and all-around Russian means, perhaps (and this you should remember), to become brother of all men, a *universal man*, if you please. (*Diary*, [August 1880], 2:979.)

In the last issue of his *Diary*, Dostoevsky, while reflecting on the general theme of universal brotherhood once more, spoke of what he calls his "Russian socialism." Here he made explicit reference to the role and importance of the Orthodox Church in this movement. Whereas previously he stressed the intermediate steps to universal brotherhood through the unification of Slavs and all Orthodox groups ("the Russian people, unfailingly must some time attain its fundamental aim, i.e., the unification of all Orthodox groups in Christ and brotherhood, without distinction between the Slavs and the other Orthodox peoples") he now extended the mission of the Orthodox Church to the whole world. His "Russian socialism" had as its ultimate goal "the establishment of an ecumenical Church on earth in so far as the earth is capable of embracing it. I am speaking of the unquenchable, inherent thirst in the Russian people for great, universal, brotherly fellowship in the name of Christ." (*Diary*, [January 1881], 2:1029.)

Dostoevsky never ceased to believe that the spiritual energies and resources needed to bring about brotherly union of mankind would emanate from the masses, not from the intelligentsia. This is indicated in part by his interpretation of Pushkin and his notion "that in the people, and only in them, we shall fully discover our Russian genius and the cognizance of its destiny, for "the essence of Christianity, its spirit and truth, are conserved and fortified in them—despite their vices—as strongly as, perhaps in no other people in the world." (*Diary* [March 1877], 2:631.)

The peasants would save Russia and, in turn, the entire world. "The salvation of Russia comes from the people," Zossima said. (*Brothers Karamazov*, 377.) They would overcome atheism and preserve Orthodoxy. It was different, however, for the upper classes because of their desire to base right and wrong on reason alone. "But God will save Russia as He has saved her many times. Salvation will come from the people, from their faith and their meekness," Zossima repeated. A third time Zossima asserted the peasants' faith in Christ. "But God will save His people, for Russia is great in her humility." (*Brothers Karamazov*, 379.) This belief remained with Dostoevsky to his dying day. In the last issue of the *Diary* he reasserted the same faith in the people:

> Here I shall repeat in my own words which I uttered long ago; the overwhelming mass of the Russian people is Orthodox; it lives by the idea of Orthodoxy in all its completeness despite the fact that rationally and scientifically they do not comprehend this idea. *Essentially*, save for this 'idea' there dwells no other in our people; every-

thing is derived from it, at least this is what the people want wholeheartedly and with deep conviction. They want precisely everything they possess and everything that is given them, to emanate exclusively from this idea. (*Diary*, [January 1881], 2:1028.)[45]

Dostoevsky expressed this theme five years earlier: the masses maintain "the firm belief that Russia exists for the sole purpose of serving Christ and protecting ecumenic orthodoxy as a whole." (*Diary*, [December 1876], 1:555.)

The Monastery and the Orthodox Ideal

If the ideal which Dostoevsky so often stresses in his *Diary* was found wanting in the masses, where could one turn to? where was the Orthodox ideal most perfectly embodied and operational? For Dostoevsky the answer was the Russian monastery; there the living image of Christ and Orthodoxy were found together.

As early as December 1869, Dostoevsky showed a special interest in monastery life and its historical figures. In *The Possessed*, Dostoevsky began the groundwork for his later characterization of Zossima, this time under the name of Tikhon. In a letter of December 26, 1869, he expressed a keen interest to learn more about the ascetical life. "The second half of my first story takes place in a monastery. I must not only see a monastery (I have seen many), but live in one." (*Pis'ma*, 2:245 [To S. A. Ivanova].)

The reputation of the monastery near Kozelsk, Optina Pustyn, was particularly inviting. According to Mochulaky, "the holiness of the monastery shone over all Russia. Legends about the Elder Ambrose—the ascetic, healer, and miracle worker—circulated among the people."[46] The celebrated intellectuals of the day who visited Optina included Gogol, Kireeveski, Solovyov, and Tolstoy.

After the death of his young son in 1878, Dostoevsky visited Optina for several talks with Father Ambrose. At this visit Dostoevsky gathered more material for the future Zossima in *The Brothers Karamazov*, in effect finding material for a portrait of the perfect man, the saint on the Russian scene. At long last he could accomplish what had earlier turned out to be less successful than he hoped, the figure of Myshkin in *The Idiot*.

Dostoevsky had earlier written to Maikov, discussing with him the characters of his then forthcoming novel, *The Possessed*. Referring to the figure of Tikhon, he wrote, "Perhaps I shall succeed in creating a majestic, authentic saint." (*Letters*, 192.) The conversations between Stavrogin and Tikhon in *The Possessed* allowed Dostoevsky to bring out the penetrating insight of this Russian elder ("At Tikhon's", 405–43). Later Dostoevsky defined an elder in the following fashion: "An elder was one who took your soul, your will, into his soul and his will. When you choose an elder, you renounce your own will and yield it to him in complete submission, complete self-abnegation." (*Brothers Karamazov*, 27.)

Tikhon was a bishop who retired to the Efimove Monastery of our Lady because of illness. He is described as a "tall, thin men of about fifty-five; he was dressed in a simple cassock and looked rather sickly. There was a vague smile on his face and his whole expression was strange and rather shy. Stavrogin had found out that Tikhon had already been living in the monastery for six years and that he received visits from the humblest peasants as well as the most famous people. Even in Petersburg he had had an ardent following of men—and even more devoted following of women." (*The Possessed*, 406–7.) When Dostoevsky began the first drafts of *The Brothers Karamazov*, he again used the name of Tikhon, but later replaced it with the Elder Zossima. Mochulsky offers a different emphasis: "Zossima is not a representative of historical Russian monasticism; he is directed toward the future as a herald of the new spiritual consciousness of the Russian people. In his religiosity there is an enraptured sense of the divinity of the world and the Godlikeness of man; he sees the mystical unity of the cosmos and its illumination by the Holy Spirit (Beauty); this is the source of his teaching that 'all men are guilty for everyone.'"[47]

In a letter to N. A. Liubimov from Ems 7/19 August 1879, Dostoevsky reveals the closeness of thought between the author and his creation.

> You can see for yourself that many of the precepts of my elder Zossima (or rather the manner of their expression) belong to his character, that is, to the artistic expression of it. I hold completely the very same ideas which he expresses, but if I personally expressed them from myself, I would express them in a different form and in a different style. It was impossible to use a different style or a differ-

ent spirit than which I gave him. Otherwise this literary character would not have been created." (*Pis'ma*, 4:91)

Dostoevsky then says that he molded the figure of Zossima after the old Russian monks and prelates who possessed a boundless faith in the future of both the moral and political missions of Russia, and asks, "Have not that Saints Sergius, Metropolitans Peter and Alexey always regarded Russia in that way?" (*Pis'ma*, 4:91–92.) Zossima shows throughout his personal convictions, the certitude of his advice, his general joyous optimism and his inspirational idealism, for instance, the notion that heaven lies hidden within all of mankind, the idea that all are responsible for the other person, and finally that men use sin and suffering to climb toward salvation in a spirit of atonement, humility and love of God.

Dostoevsky put forth his belief in the role of monastic life for Russia through the Elder Zossima, notably during his conversations with the monks. Zossima refuted the banal objection, that such a life is useless, an idle waste of time, and said:

> How surprised men would be if I were to say that from these meek monks, who yearn for solitary prayer, the salvation of Russia will come perhaps once more. For they are in truth made ready in peace and quiet 'for the day and the hour, the month and the year.' Meanwhile, in their solitude, they keep the image of Christ fair and undefiled, in the purity of God's truth, from the times of the Fathers of old, the Apostles and the martyrs. And when the time comes they will show it to the tottering creeds of the world. That is a great thought. That star will rise out of the East. (*The Brother Karamazov*, 375.)

When the problem of the monk being isolated from "the world" is broached, Zossima makes another case for the real relationship between the people and the monks:

> But we shall see which will be most zealous in the cause of brotherly love. For it is not we, but they, who are in isolation, though they don't see that. Of old, leaders of the people came from among us, and why should they not again? The same meek and humble ascetics will rise up and go out to work for the great cause. The salvation of Russia comes from the people. And the Russian monk has always been on the side of the people. We are isolated only if the people are isolated. . . . Take care of the peasant and guard his heart. Go on educating

him quietly. That's your duty as monks, for the peasant has God in his heart. (*Brothers Karamazov,* 377.)

The Unity of Church and State

Dostoevsky's *Brothers Karamazov* was the climax of a prolific career of literary creativity and a powerful summary of what Christian living entailed for the individual; but it also marked a high point in Dostoevsky's reflection on Christian society. Like Europe, Russia was in ferment. What kind of society would evolve was uncertain. Dostoevsky hoped for a civilization that was absorbed and engrossed in Christian truth, both in a theoretical precept and functional-operational way. His contribution was only in most general terms, one that called for much more thought and adaptation to the structures of society that would actually evolve in the decades ahead. Some would call his "Russian socialism" a utopia based on unrealistic hopes and an overidealistic conception of human potentiality.

In the chapter entitled "So Be It! So Be It!" Dostoevsky ventured into the possibilities of a new society based on the central truths of his own Orthodox ideas. The new idea concerned the relationship between Church and State. Païssy, Ivan, in dialog with Zossima, the librarian Father Iosif, Father Païssy, and Miüsov, suggested the blending of Church and State into one being, a theocratic state, better still, a theocracy on earth. He suggested that "the Church ought to include the whole State, and not simply to occupy a corner in it, and, if this is, for some reason, impossible at present, then it ought, in reality, to be set up as the direct and chief aim of the future development of Christian society!" "Perfectly true," Father Païssy, the "silent and learned monk" rejoins with "fervor and decision while Miüsov cries out impatiently, "the purest Ultramontanism!" (*Brothers Karamazov,* 69.)

Ivan, voicing Dostoevsky's ideas, affirms that "Every earthly State should be, in the end, completely transformed into the Church and should become nothing else but a Church, rejecting every purpose incongruous with the aims of the Church." (*Brothers Karamazov,* 70.) Father Païssy then recapitulates the general trend of the arguments and concludes: "But Russians hopes and conceptions demand not that the Church should pass as from a lower into a higher type into the State, but, on the contrary, that the State should end by being worthy to become only the Church and nothing else. So be it! So be it!" (*Brothers Karamazov,* 71.)

After a lengthy discussion of the merits of the old and new society, and their influence on the morality of the people, notably criminals, Fr. Zossima suggests that while the ideas are to be cherished and worthy, they are still somewhere in the future and that "the Christian society now is not ready and is only resting on some seven righteous men, but as they are never lacking, it will continue still unshaken in expectation of its complete transformation from a society almost heathen in character into a single universal and all-powerful Church. So be it, so be it!" (*Brothers Karamazov,* 74.)

Father Païssy concludes the main thrust of the dialog by forecasting a great future for Russia under the general notions of this new type of society. "Understand, the Church is not to be transformed into the State. That is Rome and its dream. That is the third temptation of the devil. On the contrary, the State is transformed into the Church, will ascend and become a Church over the whole world— which is the complete opposite of Ultramontanism and Rome, and your interpretation, and is only the glorious destiny ordained for the Orthodox Church. This star will arise in the east!" (*Brothers Karamazov,* 75.)

Commentators recognize Dostoevsky's constant concern with the ramifications of freedom in human existence, and his absorption by the Russian Orthodox Church. "His passion for freedom was equal to Khomyakov's, and his conviction that the state would eventually be transformed by true faith and become the church, went beyond the view of the Slavophiles, although comparable ideas had been suggested by Ivan Kireevskii and Kireevskii's associates."[48]

Solovyov defends Dostoevsky's Romantic vision of the new Church: "Dostoevsky did not have any kind of theological pretension, and so we do not have the right to look for any kind of logical definitions on its nature from him. But preaching a Church as a societal ideal, he expressed an entirely clear and definite demand, so clear and defined (though directly opposite), as that demand which was manifested by European socialism (and so in his last diary Dostoevsky could call the people's faith in the Church our Russian socialism)."[49]

Solovyov relates a story of Dostoevsky's wherein he compares Russia to a vision of John in the Apocalypse of a woman in labor, surrounded by the sun, about to bring forth the son of man; the wife represents Russia and the one to be borne by her is the new word that Russia is to give the world.[50] Dostoevsky often writes on the Orthodox ideal, often implying a discrepancy between the real and the ideal. Although Dostoevsky was not what one would today call a "churchy" man nor an "institutional" man, he criticized the Church itself very little. Occasionally, it is true, he makes sarcastic or pungent comments on a few topics. For instance, writing in the 1873 edition of the *Diary* he prods the clergy with the following remark: "Our priests, too—it is rumored—begin to awake. It is said that our clergy began long ago to reveal signs of life. We read with humble gratification the admonitions of the ecclesiastical masters in churches, regarding the virtues of preaching and of the moral way of living. According to all reports, our spiritual leaders are resolutely beginning to compose sermons and are getting ready to deliver them." (*Diary* [1873], 1:64.) Then in the January 1876 issue, the question of money is broached. "Most disturbing facts were reported to the effect that there were religious teachers who, by the dozens and wholesale, deserted the schools and refused to teach in them without an increase in their salaries. No doubt, 'he who works has got to be paid,' but this everlasting howling about a raise in compensation hurts one's ear and tortures one's heart." (*Diary*, [January 1876], 1:180.)

In an isolated cryptic remark, Dostoevsky says that the Church has been paralyzed since the time of Peter the Great. (*Biographia*, 356.)[51] But "The star will rise in the East" is the culminating expression of Dostoevsky's faith in Orthodoxy.

Conclusion: The Prevalance of the Star

This provocative symbol comes from Matthew's second chapter on the coming of Christ. The wise men or astrologers who would search out the portents governing the world were amazed by the coming of a savior. Dostoevsky, first linking the Russian masses with Orthodoxy and then identifying Orthodoxy with the transformation of Russian society and the universalization of Christian brotherhood the world over, forged an attractive élan for Russia and a nineteenth-century world that was full of conflict and insecurity.

THREE

DOSTOEVSKY AND THE CATHOLIC PAX ROMANA

First Trip to the West (1862)

On June 7, 1862, Dostoevsky gave in to the "powerful, magic, compelling appeal" of Europe, and fulfilled an old childhood wish (*Winter Notes*, 47). Feeling secure after selling the publication rights for his *House of the Dead* and entrusting the management of *Vremya* to his brother Michael, Dostoevsky left for the West. He was ecstatic about the adventure:

> Good Lord! How much I expected from that trip! . . . I'll see everything, I'll go every place. And from all that I see I'll form an overall picture, I'll see the entire 'land of sacred wonders' as a whole, in a bird's-eye view, like the Promised Land seen in perspective from a mountain top. . . . Here I am about to see Europe, I who had been dreaming of it in vain for almost forty years, I who since my sixteenth year, like Nekrasov's Belopyatkin, had seriously 'wished to fly off to Switzerland' but had not flown off. And here I am finally entering 'the land of sacred wonders,' the land for which I have been languishing so long, in which I have believed so staunchly. (*Winter Notes*, 36, 47.)

Though Dostoevsky visited many cities—Geneva, Lucerne, Baden-Baden, Berlin, Cologne, Dresden, Wiesbaden, Tournai, Paris, Genoa, Florence, Milan, and Venice—in the short span of two and a half months, his stay in Western Europe was crucial in the development of his philosophical, political, and religious views. "Clearly his first visit abroad cannot be dismissed as just another biographical fact in Dostoevsky's life. He carried with him an idealized picture of his own countrymen; by contrast his observations in Europe seemed to strengthen his faith in the future high destiny of Russia if it could be kept free from the poison of the West."[1]

Dostoevsky Appalled by Europe

The conditions in Europe appalled Dostoevsky; this is reflected in every page of his *Winter Notes*, a rambling commentary on European culture spiced with much small talk and carefully aimed barbs against the West.

His first impression of Berlin, for instance, is bitter, for there he developed a liver ailment and encountered nasty weather and rough traveling conditions. Berlin, he objects, is too much of a copy of St. Petersburg, with the same "colorless streets, the same odors." He also relates it requires "special pains to accustom" himself to the Germans in large groups and registers a complaint against the "repulsive" nature of Dresden women (*Winter Notes*, 37–38).

Dostoevsky begins his exposé of the French with a jab made by Denis Fonvizin on his own tour through Europe about eight decades earlier: "The Frenchman has no sense, and he would consider it the greatest personal misfortune if he did." (*Winter Notes*, 45.)[2] Dostoevsky's comment is enlightening:

> I'll bet that his heart was bursting with delight as he composed it. And who knows? Perhaps all of us who have followed Fonvizin, three or four generations in a row, have read it not without a certain enjoyment. All sentences that bring foreigners down a peg contain something undeniably delectable for us Russians even today. Only covertly, of course, and in some cases we ourselves are not aware of it. This smacks of a certain vengeance for something unfortunate in our past. Perhaps this is an unfortunate attitude, but I am somehow convinced that it exists in almost every one of us. (*Winter Notes*, 45.)

In a chapter full of irony and sarcasm entitled "Baal," Dostoevsky trades punches with Paris, London, and all of Europe in general. Here he refers to the trends of "orderliness" that envelop the atmosphere: "And what regimentation! understand me: not so much external regimentation, which is of no consequence (relatively, of course), as a colossal internal and spiritual regimentation, coming from the very soul. Paris, it would seem, wants to contract, to dwindle with love, to shrink with tenderness. There is no comparing it with London in this respect." (*Winter Notes*, 88–89.)

Conditions in England

In London, which Dostoevsky found "so huge and garish," he observes

> the same relentless, vague, chronic struggle, the mortal struggle be-
> tween the individualistic basis of the whole Western world and the
> necessity of finding some way to live together, of finding some way
> to fashion a community and set up house all in the same anthill; it
> may be only an anthill, but we had better get organized without de-
> vouring each other, or else we'll become cannibals! In this respect,
> however, you observe the same thing as in Paris: the same frantic
> struggle to preserve the status quo, to wring from oneself all one's
> desires and hopes, to curse one's future, in which even the leaders
> of progress do not have enough faith perhaps, and to worship Baal.
> (*Winter Notes*, 89.)

London, Dostoevsky writes in a still pertinent critique, is a city of people bustling here and there amidst the screech and roar of machines. London encompasses the polluted Thames and the black air that is saturated with coal dust as well as

> those terrible sections of the city like Whitechapel with its half-
> naked, savage, and hungry population. A city with its millions and
> its worldwide commerce, the Crystal Palace, the International Ex-
> position. . . . Ah, yes, the Expositions is astonishing. You sense the
> terrible force which has drawn these people without number from
> all over the world into a single herd; you become aware of a colossal

idea; you sense that something has been achieved that here there is victory and triumph. . . . 'Isn't this the ultimate?' Could this in fact be the 'one fold?'. . . . You look at these hundreds of thousands, these millions of people humbly streaming here from all over the face of the earth—people come with a single thought, quietly, relentlessly, mutely thronging into this colossal palace, and you feel that something final has taken place here, that something has come to an end. It is like a Biblical picture, something out of Babylon, a prophecy from the Apocalypse coming to pass before your eyes. You sense that it would require great and everlasting spiritual determination and fortitude in order not to submit, not to capitulate before the impression, not to bow to what is and not to deify Baal, that is, not to accept the material world as your ideal. (*Winter Notes*, 90–91.)

Dostoevsky delights in providing dramatic contrasts for his readers. Here, particularly, he describes the colossal feats of human nature in the international exhibition. Man is almost ready to bow down to his own creation. At the same time this same portion of the human race is ready to seek "salvation in gin and debauchery and begins to believe that everything is as it ought to be." (*Winter Notes*, 92.) There in London, he writes,

on Saturday nights a half-million workers, male and female, together with their children, flood the city like a sea, flocking especially in certain sections, and celebrate the Sabbath all night until five in the morning; that is, they stuff themselves and drink like animals, enough to last the week. . . . Everything is drunk, but drunk without joy, and somber and heavy and strangely silent. Only occasionally do swearing and bloody brawls trouble this auspicious, dismal, oppressive silence. They all race against time to drink themselves insensate. (*Winter Notes*, 92–93.)

Dostoeveky also describes his experience in Haymarket where mothers bring their young daughters to "do business"; he centers his attention on a "filthy barefooted, emaciated, hollow-cheeked" girl who is full of black and blue marks. Dostoeveky gives the girl a half-shilling and she runs off.

France: Individualism versus Fraternity

Dostoevsky continues his biting commentary on the West by moving on to France in his sixth chapter essay "on the Bourgeoisie." He portrays the French bourgeoisie as being ill at ease in everyday life, feeling internally that something is awry while dreaming of the beautiful life. The Parisian, moreover, is money-mad. His principal passion is to accumulate a fortune. But Dostoevsky centers the brunt of his commentary on what he believes to be the absence of human brotherhood in the West, notably in France:

> The Westerner speaks of fraternity as of a great motivating force of humankind, and does not understand that it is impossible to obtain fraternity if it does not exist in reality. What is to be done? Fraternity must be obtained at any cost. But as it happens it is impossible to create fraternity, for it creates itself, comes of itself, exists in nature. But in French nature, and in Occidental nature in general, it is not present; you find there instead a principle of individualism, a principle of isolation, of intense self-preservation, of personal gain, of self-determination of the *I*, of opposing this *I* to all nature and the rest of mankind as an independent, autonomous principle entirely equal and equivalent to all that exists outside itself. Well, fraternity could scarcely arise from such an attitude. (*Winter Notes*, 110–11.)

Return to Russia and Second Trip to Europe

Dostoevsky returned to Russia after his first trip, more hostile than ever toward the West. But he did not stay away from the "degenerate" West for long. In May 1863 the Russian government suppressed *Vremya* due to a misunderstanding over an article on the Polish question written by Strakhov.[3] His wife ill and not in the best of health himself, Dostoeveky borrowed money from the Fund for Needy Authors and left for his second visit to Europe.

Dostoevsky's traveling companion for two months was Pauline Suslova. He was so infatuated with her by the spring of 1863 that he could not spend a day without her.[4] Dostoevsky's funds were quickly depleted, and he had to write to his brother for assistance. On one occasion he and Pauline were so desperate that they had to pawn their watches. During this period Dostoevsky became allured by the gambling table, a passion that he could not control until 1871.[5]

Death of First Wife

On April 16, 1864 Dostoevsky's wife died of consumption. The marriage had been unhappy; certainly he felt relief and remorse at her death. But on June 10, his brother Michael also died and Dostoevsky precipitously assumed the debts and support of his brother's family and relatives. Unable to handle these financial obligations, he left for his third trip to Europe in late July 1865.

While at Wiesbaden, Dostoevsky went on another gambling spree at the roulette table and lost every cent he owned. Thanks to a fifty thaler loan from Ivan Turgenev, he got on his feet again. But this incident began the friction between the two writers that would last to the end of their lives. Before this time, the two writers were aware of each other's works and corresponded on various occasions though there was no great substance to their relationship.

Crime and Punishment

Dostoevsky returned to Russia in November 1865 ready to sell the rights to his new novel, *Crime and Punishment*. The following year the novel was published serially in *Russkiy Vestnik* and in book form. Dostoevsky was still taken up with the *volitional* animal, the schismatic superman, Raskolnikov. The work has no direct reference to the West, but there is one slight insinuation when the mother Pulcheria writes to her son: "Do you still say your prayers, Rodya, and believe in the mercy of our Creator and our Redeemer? I am afraid in my heart that you may have been visited by the new spirit of infidelity that is abroad today; if it is so, I pray for you." (*Crime and Punishment*, 35.)

Second Marriage; The Gambler

Toward the end of 1866, Dostoevsky began work on *The Gambler*, a subject he was unfortunately already only too familiar with, and engaged a young lady to dictate his work to, Anna G. Snitkin. They were married on February 15, 1867, and left for Europe on April 14, his fourth trip abroad. The year was full of despair intensified with bouts of epilepsy, uninhibited gambling, and endless pawning of clothes and personal possessions. If it were not for the creditors, he and his wife would have returned to Russia at once.

Quarrel with Turgenev

The highly excitable nature of Dostoevsky and his ideological embitterment is reflected in the quarrel that ensued with Turgenev. Dostoevsky was naturally envious of a man like Turgenev who could write in comparative financial security while he had to scrimp and strain to make ends meet. Turgenev, on the other hand, recognized the significant talent that Dostoevsky possessed, but he felt his world usually unnecessarily alien to himself. He referred to Dostoevsky as "the Russian Marquis de Sade" and "the most vicious Christian" he had ever met.[6]

Turgenev's Smoke

The deepest part of this grudge stemmed from the diametrically opposed ideologies of the two writers; this is best seen in the novel *Smoke*, which Turgenev published in 1867. The message of this work was that Russia had much to learn from the West and that her borrowings to the moment had been quite superficial. Dostoevsky was personally galled by the main thesis of *Smoke*, notably where Turgenev points out that

> To look down upon the West from the mystic height of an ignorant and pompous nationalism, as the Slavophiles do, is folly as outrageous as to worship, like the radical set, the peasant's *armyak* (coat) and to expect sweetness and light to stream from his cockroach-infested hut. Culturally speaking, there is nothing either in Russia's past or present to be proud of. Its future depends on the people's ability to choose these elements of Western civilization that are most suited to Russia's needs and to make them their own. (*Smoke*, 254.)

In the novel itself Russian life is seen not through the eyes of Litvinov, a decent and ordinary person, but through those of Potugin the Westerner. In a passage where the future of Russia is discussed, Potugin remarks

> And of course they'll have a dig at 'the rotten West' by the way. It's a queer thing if you come to think of it—this West beats us on every point, and yet it's rotten! . . . At the moment there is nothing at all, and in the course of ten centuries Russia has produced nothing of its own either in government or in law or in science or in art, or even in crafts. . . . Look at the peasant! That's where it will all come from. All other idols have been shattered, so let us believe in the peasant. (*Smoke*, 35–39.)

In a telling blow to the slavophile viewpoint toward the end of the novel, Turgenev pictures Litvinov in a pensive and puzzled mood: "'Smoke, smoke,' he repeated several times; and it suddenly seemed to him that everything was smoke: everything—his own life, Russian life, everything human, especially everything Russian." (*Smoke*, 225.)

In particular, Dostoevsky deeply resented the leading idea of Turgenev's novel, that "if Russia were destroyed by an earthquake and vanished from the globe, it would mean no loss to humanity—it would not even be noticed." (*Letters*, 121.) Turgenev, for his part, resented Dostoevsky's castigation of the people and conditions in Germany. Turgenev replied to these jabs by saying: "When you speak like that, you offend me personally. You know that I have settled down here finally, that I consider myself a German, not a Russian, and am proud of it."[7]

Dostoevsky elaborated on his disagreement with Turgenev in a letter to his wife:

> And what have they—the Turgenevs, Herzens, Outins, Cherynshevskys—given us? Instead of the highest divine beauty, at which they spit, all of them are so filthily egotistical, so shameless, irritable, light-mindedly proud that one simply can't make out what they hope for and who will follow them. Turgenev abused Russia and Russians disgustingly, terribly. But this is what I observed: all these little liberals and progressives, still pre-eminently of Belinsky's school, find it their principal pleasure and satisfaction to rail at Russia, the difference only being that the followers of Chernyshevsky revile Russia plainly, and frankly wish her to go under (above all, to go under!) but these offshoots add that they *love Russia*. And yet not only is everything that is in the least original in Russia hateful to them, so that they deny it and instantly delight to turn it into caricature; but if you were at last to present to them actually a fact, which could neither be refuted nor caricatured, but which even they could not fail to agree, then it seems that they would be tormentingly, achingly, desperately unhappy.[8]

During his four-year exile abroad, besides making pitiful requests for additional funds, one of Dostoevsky's preoccupations is the intolerable, "vile" people in Europe. Geneva, a dull, gloomy town, he relates, is "detestable, and I grossly deceived myself about it. My attacks recur almost every week here; and also I sometimes have a peculiar, troubling fluttering of the heart." The people are "boastful," and "everything is ugly here, utterly rotten and expensive. Everybody is drunk!" (*Pis'ma* (October 9/21, 1867) 2:46.)

Friendship with Maikov

This is one of many letters Dostoevsky wrote to Appollon Maikov with whom he had struck up a friendship in 1843. While abroad, Maikov served as a bridge to Russia, and Dostoevsky entrusted his money matters to him. Dostoevsky expressed his appreciation of Maikov in a letter of May 15/27, 1869: "But you are right; for of all those whom I have happened to meet and to live with for the last forty-eight years, you and you alone I consider as a man after my heart." (*Pis'ma* [May 15/27, 1869], 2:189.) In another Genevan letter to Maikov in the winter of 1867–68, Dostoevsky complains that "a workman here is not worth the little finger of our workman. It is ludicrous to see and to hear it all. The customs are savage; oh, if you only knew what they consider good and bad here. Their inferiority of development: the drunkenness, the thieving, the paltry swindling, that have become the rule in their commerce!" (*Pis'ma* 2:64.)

Dense, ugly, stupid are words that Dostoevsky used to describe the people and conditions in Germany. He states, moreover, that he would have laughed out loud if someone had told him of the things waiting for him in Europe. His wife offers similar sentiments, stating that she was looking forward to the trip with great anticipation, but she had a change of heart. "I had come to hate them almost. Everything abroad—religion, language, people, customs, manners— seemed to me not only foreign, but hostile." (*Letters and Reminiscences*, 104.) Dostoevsky's wife reports that her husband stated that "nowhere in the world were there so many rogues as in Germany."[9]

Dostoevsky and Russian Emigres

One sight that especially irked Dostoevsky was other Russians wandering about or settling down in Europe. He referred to these people as "utter negators of Russia. They became destroyers of Russia, enemies of Russia! This is what it meant to be ground from a Russian into a genuine European, to become at last a true son of civilization." (*Diary* [June 1876], 1:357.)

In a rare expression of self-criticism, Dostoevsky stated that "only one thing can be said of the whole mass of us: as soon as we pass we assume a striking resemblance to those unfortunate little dogs that run around in search of their master." (*WinterNotes*, 76.) Writing from Florence to his niece Sofia Alexandrovna on January 25/ February 6, 1869, Dostoevsky again expresses his exasperation with his own countrymen. "In three months, we shall have been two years abroad. In my opinion, it is worse than deportation to Siberia. I mean that quite seriously and without any exaggeration. I cannot understand the Russians abroad." (*Pis'ma* 2:160.)

While in Ems for a cure during the summer of 1874, Dostoevsky continued to criticize the apparent aimlessness of his fellow Russians. "Half of the people here are Russians, There's nothing to talk about them. It is always depressing to see Russians knocking about abroad; such emptiness, idleness and general smugness." (*Pis'ma* 3:116.)

In the same letter he speaks of a certain Father Tachalov, a Russian priest from Wiesbaden, "a supercilious beast who comes here on Mondays, but I squashed him and he soon disappeared. He is an intriguer and a swindler. He would sell everything, even Christ." More revolting, he relates, the same priest boasts of converting Catholics, "and the beast manages to be convincing although he is as stupid as a log and by his ignorance disgraces our church before strangers. (*Pis'ma* 3:116–17.)

Homesickness and Fear of Artistic Decline

Dostoevsky was hardly settled in Europe when he began to express his homesickness. Much more deeply was the question of losing his talent. This fear came to the surface innumerable times. In a letter to Maikov from Geneva on August 16/28,1867, he remarks: "How is it possible to endure this living abroad? By God, without home, it's sheer torture! To travel for six months or a year is fine. But to travel, as I do, without knowing or even guessing when one will get home again, is very bad and grievous. The mere thought of it is hard to bear. I need Russia for my writing, I speak of no life but that. I am like a fish out of water; I am losing all my energies, all my faculties." (*Pis'ma* 2:25.)

Writing to his niece Sofia from Florence on March 8/20, 1869, concerning a new novel on atheism he makes the same point: "I must absolutely be in Russia, I must see and hear everything, I must take my part in Russian life; and besides, the work would take at least two years, I can't do it here, and must therefore write something else in the meantime." (*Pis'ma* 2:175.

The fear of losing his talent was so deep that it even made a deep impression on his wife. She wrote, "Fyodor so often spoke of the certain 'ruin' of his talent, if he remained any longer abroad, and was so tormented by the thought that he would not be able to keep his family, that, as I listened to him, I too was driven to despair."[10]

The Idiot, The Devils: *Answer to Turgenev*

Toward the end of 1867, Dostoevsky began work on *The Idiot*, which was published serially in the *Russkiy Vestnik* and in book form the following year. In 1870 he began work on his next major novel, *The Devils*, in part an answer to Turgenev's treatment of nihilism in *Fathers and Sons*. The liberal temper as exemplified in Stepan Trofimovich undermined society. In this work Dostoevsky nursed the coals of the feud by caricaturing Turgenev in the person of Karmazinov, a pompous and foolish writer who declared his sympathy to a clandestine movement and expressed his admiration for the "potency of the message."

European Opposition to Russia

With the publication of *The Idiot* and *The Devils* and the two succeeding novels, Dostoevsky continued to complain and criticize the West. Instead of emphasizing his own personal reactions to his enforced exile, he began to describe Europe's attitudes toward Russia. A major theme of the *Diary*, initiated in 1873, is the conviction that the West was inexorably opposed, indeed hostile, to Russia. Furthermore, this view was so firmly entrenched that Europe simply could not understand the true intentions and motivations of Russia. Writing for the *Diary* in April 1876, Dostoevsky stated: "It is difficult to conceive to what extent she is afraid of us. And if she is afraid of us, she must be hating us. Europe has always extraordinarily disliked us; she never did like us; she never regarded us as one of her own—as Europeans—but always has viewed us as disagreeable strangers. This is why, at times, she is fond of consoling herself with the thought that Russia supposedly is 'as yet impotent.'" (*Diary* [April 1876], 1:295.)

Dostoevsky continued his critique by stating why it was to Russia's advantage not to have proved a major military power in the Crimean War. Otherwise Russia would have had to face the entire armed might of Europe:

> Having perceived how powerful we are, everybody in Europe would then forthwith have risen against us with fanatical hatred. Of course, had they been crushed, they would have signed a peace treaty disadvantageous to them, but never could any peace have been achieved in reality. They would immediately begin to prepare themselves for a new war aiming at the annihilation of Russia, and the principal point is that they would have had the support of the whole world. For example, in this event the year 1864 would not have cost us merely an exchange of caustic diplomatic notes: on the contrary, a wholesale crusade against Russia would have ensued. (*Diary* [April 1876], 1:295.)

Dostoevsky may have fluctuated in his appraisal of Europe, but he never changed his conviction that Europe opposed the best interests of Russia. In the January 1881 issue of the *Diary*, he reaffirms his old position: "Europe is ready to praise us, to stroke our heads, but she does not recognize us as hers, she despises us, whether secretly or openly; she considers us as an inferior race. At times, she feels aversion to us, especially when we fling ourselves on her neck with brotherly embraces." (*Diary* [January 1881], 2:1047.)

By the middle and late seventies, according to Dostoevsky, the tables had been turned in favor of Russia. While the Crimean War had shaken the lethargy of Russia, the West had brought forth divisive interests and goals. In the role of prophet, Dostoevsky then forecast the demise of the West, which had so hated Russia down through the centuries. "And the world is threatened by many a thing: at no time in the past has Europe been loaded with such elements of ill will as at present. It seems that everything is undermined and loaded with powder, and is just waiting for the first spark." (*Diary* [February 1877], 1:258.)

European Materialism

Europe had lost all sense of proper values and perspectives; their morality had worn itself out. Europe, according to Dostoevsky, was merely living on a day-to-day basis, not knowing what would happen to her next:

> Let it be noted that Europe has unquestionably reached the point where she treasures most of the current gain, the gain of the actual moment—even at any price,—since over there, they are living merely from day to day, by the present minute only, and they even do not know themselves what is going to happen to them tomorrow. However, we—Russia—we still believe in something lasting, which moulds itself in Russia, and therefore we seek permanent and essential gains. It is also for this reason that we, as a political organism, have always believed in eternal morality, and not in a relative one, good but for a few days. (*Diary* [February 1877], 2:608.)

The Doom of the West

In 1877 Dostoevsky repeatedly returned to the theme of the vast cataclysms awaiting Europe. In the January issue of the *Diary* he referred to the restless state of Europe where the time had come "for something sempiternal, millenarian, for that which has been moulding itself in the world ever since the beginning of its civilization." (*Diary* [January 1877], 2:562.)

In November he restated the same thesis. "The point is that we are on the eve of the greatest and most violent events and revolutions in Europe—and this *without exaggeration*." In the same article he wrote, "Yes, immense cataclysms are awaiting Europe, perturbations which the human mind refuses to believe, conceiving their realization as something fantastic."(*Diary* [November 1877], 2:908.)

Just less than a year before his death he wrote with the same certainty that "Europe is on the eve of a general and dreadful collapse."

Europe is an ant-hill he says, and "this ant-hill is utterly undermined." (*Diary* [August 1880], 2:1003.)

Dostoevsky saved the most dramatic expression of his view of the doomed West for two of his leading figures in *A Raw Youth* and *The Brothers Karamazov*. For his part, Versilov relates his dream in a sleepy German town:

> It was by then quite evening; through the green of the flowers that stood in the windows of my little room, broke slanting rays [Dostoevsky's favorite symbol of illumination and inspiration, that is, divine grace], that flooded me with light. And then, my dear— that setting sun of the first day of European civilization which I had seen in my dream was transformed for me at once on waking, into the setting sun of the last day of civilization! One seemed to hear the death knell ringing over Europe in those days. I am not speaking of the war and the Tuileries; apart from that, I knew that all would pass away, the whole face of the old world of Europe—sooner or later, but I, as a Russian European, could not accept it. . . . There all was strife and logic; there the Frenchman was nothing but a Frenchman, the German was nothing but a German, and this more intensely so then at any time in their whole history; consequently never had the Frenchmen done so much harm to France, or the German to Germany, as just at that time! . . . They are doomed to strife for a long time yet, because they are still too German and French, and have not yet finished struggling in those national characters. And I regret the destruction that must come before they have finished. (*Raw Youth*, 462–65.)

In a telling blow to the West, Versilov is asked: "Tell me, did Europe bring you back to life again?" In return he gives the startling reply: "Europe bring me back to life? Why, I went to bury Europe! (*Raw Youth*, 39.)

In *The Brothers Karamazov*, Ivan makes a provocative revelation to his brother Alyosha: "I want to travel in Europe, Alyosha, I shall set off from here. And yet I know that I am going to a graveyard, but it's a most precious graveyard, that's what it is! (*Brothers Karamazov*, 274.)

With his total disenchantment with the West, Dostoevsky began to cast his gaze to the East. Perhaps Russia's destiny was to be fulfilled there. In June 1876 he spoke of the future acquisition of Constantinople, "second Rome." This was not the last occasion he looked longingly at Constantinople. In January 1881, just before his death, he foretold that "we shall go to Asia as Masters," whereas "we were hangers-on and slaves" in Europe. (*Diary*, [January 1881], 2:1048.)

Critique of Socialism

In stating that Europe was a graveyard, precious as it might be, Dostoevsky summed up his critique of the West. All during the seventies he had attempted to penetrate the ideological background or spirit of the times in the West. In the *Diary* and *The Brothers Karamazov*, Dostoevsky added to the foundations he had built with *Winter Notes*, *The Devils*, and *The Idiot* by attacking the degenerating spiritual milieu of Europe. Logically, this ideological critique began with an analysis of socialism.

Dostoevsky was well acquainted with much of the theory of nineteenth-century socialism. He paid eight years of his life in Siberia for allowing himself to be tinged with its evil effects. Chastened by his Siberian experience and his subsequent exiles spent in the West, socialism thereafter received the full wrath from his pen. Above all, socialism was doomed from the start because it was inextricably attached to the destruction of Christianity. As he expresses himself in *The Brothers Karamazov*, "socialism is not merely the labor question, it is before all things the atheistic question, the question of the form taken by atheism today, the question of the tower of Babel built without God, not to mount to Heaven from earth but to set up Heaven on earth." (*Brothers Karamazov*, 26)

Socialism and Atheism

Dostoevsky viewed the direct identification of atheism and socialism in his early youth through the personal life of Vissarion Belinsky,

> who believed to the degree of delusion and without any reflex, in the new moral foundations of socialism (which, however, up to the present revealed none but abominable perversions of nature and common sense). Here was nothing but rapture. Still, as a socialist, he had to destroy Christianity in the first place. He knew that the revolution must necessarily begin with atheism. He had to dethrone that reli-

gion whence the moral foundations of the society rejected by him had sprung up. Family, property, personal moral responsibility— these he denied radically. . . . As a socialist, he was duty bound to destroy the teaching of Christ, to call it fallacious and ignorant philanthropy, doomed by modern science and economic tenets. (*Diary* [1873], 1:6–7.)

Dostoevsky repeated this idea in *The Possessed* where he has Shatov reportedly saying that "if an uprising were started in Russia, it would have to begin with atheism." *The Possessed*, 214.) Dostoevsky offers his own reflections on the temporary attachment to the "truth" and "holiness" of the regenerated world to come during his association with the Petrashevsky circle.

But at that time the affair was conceived in a most rosy and paradisaically moral light. Verily, socialism in its embryo used to be compared by some of its ringleaders with Christianity and was regarded as a mere corrective to, and improvement of, the latter, in conformity with the tendencies of the age and civilization. All these new ideas of those days carried to us, in Petersburg, a great appeal; they seemed holy in the highest degree and moral, and—most important of all— cosmopolitan, the future law of all mankind in its totality. . . . All these convictions about the immorality of the very foundations (Christian) of modern society, the immorality of religion, family, right of property; all these ideas about the elimination of nationalities in the name of universal brotherhood of men, about the contempt for one's native country, as an obstacle to universal progress, and so on, and so forth—all these constituted such influences as we were unable to overcome and which, contrariwise, swayed our hearts and minds in the name of some magnanimity. At any rate, the theme seemed lofty and far above the level of the then prevailing conceptions, and precisely this was tempting. (*Diary* [1873], 1:148–49.)

Time and time again Dostoevsky reiterates his warning against atheistic socialism. In the *Diary* for November 1877 he declares that "socialism has for its aim the solution of the destinies of mankind not in accord with Christ but without God and Christ." (*Diary*, [November 1877], 2:906.) He has Shatov declare in *The Possessed*:

In its very essence, socialism is godless—it proclaimed in its very first statement that it aims at an organization that does not presuppose

God; that is, an organization based on the principles of reason and science exclusively. But reason and science have always performed, and still perform, only an auxiliary function in the life of peoples, and it will be like that till the end of time. Nations are formed and moved by some other force whose origin is unknown and unaccountable. That force is the unquenchable will to reach an end and, at the same time, the denial of this end. It is the force of an incessant and unwavering affirmation of life and a denial of death. It is the spirit of life, 'river of water of life' as the Scriptures call it, the drying up of which is threatened in the Apocalypse. Some philosophers claim it is based on an aesthetic, others on an ethical principle, but I call it simply the search for God. (*The Possessed*, 236–37.)

Dostoevsky was convinced that the leaders of socialism, as atheists, would lead all societies into the direction opposite to progress and humanity. By promising false hopes for a new society based on scientific laws and scientific principles, it would inevitably fill the world with a spirit of antagonistic inhumanity. Moreover, he feared that this spirit—already so deeply ingrained in Europe—might spread and catch fire in Russia itself.

Perhaps I may be told that these gentlemen do not in any manner teach villainy; that if Strauss, for example, hates Christ and made it the business of his whole life to spit upon and scoff at Christianity, he nevertheless adores humankind as a whole, and his teaching is as lofty and as noble as it can be. It is very possible that all this is true, and that the aims of all modern leaders of European progressives are philanthropic and grand. Still I firmly believe that if all those modern, sublime teachers be given ample opportunity to destroy the old society and to build it up anew, there would result such a darkness, such chaos, something so coarse, so blind, so inhuman, that the entire edifice would crumble away to the accompaniment of the maledictions of mankind, even before it would finally have been constructed. The human mind, once having rejected Christ, may attain extraordinary results. This is an axiom. Europe, in the persons of her highest intellectual representatives, renounces Christ, while we, as is known, are obligated to imitate Europe. (*Diary* 1:150–51.)

In 1861 the revolutionary Peter Zaichnevsky spoke of "the glorious future of Russia, to whose lot it had fallen to be the first country to achieve the glorious work of socialism."[11] Dostoevsky offered his views on "Russian socialism" to N. A. Liubimov in a letter of June 11, 1879:

> For our Russian socialism, stupid (but terrible because the youth are with it)—here is a warning, and an urgent one it seems: bread, the tower of Babel (that is, the future kingdom of socialism) and the complete subjugation of the freedom of conscience—that is what the desperate negativist and atheist arrives at. The difference consists in that our socialists (and they are not only the underground nihilists—you know that) are conscious Jesuits and liars who will not confess that their ideal is the violation of man's conscience and the reduction of mankind to the level of a herd of cattle. (*Pis'ma* 4:58.)

Though Dostoevsky felt that socialism had already "corroded Europe," in his view the leaders of European socialism were mere dreamers and speculators who leaned on the false hopes of a new science to establish immovable principles for a new community of man. But science, he maintains, is ill-prepared to fulfill its goal. "It is difficult to conceive that it should possess such a thorough knowledge of human nature as to devise unmistakably new laws for the social organism. Since, however, this problem cannot be held in suspense and in a state of oscillation, there naturally arises the question: is science ready for this particular task *forthwith*, even if in its future development this task be not exceeding the efficacy of science?" (*Diary* [March 1876], 1:252.)

Besides failing on the methodological level, Dostoevsky felt that there was another important component that would insure the nonviability of socialism in the West, namely the human factor. This conviction dates from Dostoevsky's first trip abroad. Concluding that there is neither the notion nor the reality of brotherhood in the West, Dostoevsky asks: "What, then, can the Socialist do, if there is no principle of brotherhood in the Westerner but, on the contrary, an individualist isolationist instinct which stands aloof and demands its rights with sword in hand? Observing that there is no fraternity around, the socialist tries to talk fraternity into people." (*Winter Notes*, 114.)

In the absence of the basic ingredient, brotherhood, Dostoevsky pictures the socialist reverting to the tools of logic, precision, and science to make his case. Everything is measured for future categorization and distribution.

The frantic Socialist sets desperately to work on the future fraternity, defining it, calculating its size and weight, enticing you with its advantages, explaining, teaching, telling of the profit each stands to gain from the fraternity and just how much each will win; he determines what each personality will look like and what burden each will represent, and determines in advance the division of earthly wealth; what part each one will merit and how much each in return must pay to the community at the expense of his individuality. (*Winter Notes*, 114.)

Roman Catholicism and Socialism

France, Dostoevsky believed, was the heart of the socialist movement. In that country the picture was most clear, the crucial factor being that France, paradoxically, was considered the Catholic country par excellence. And thus Dostoevsky's critique of socialism really resulted in a propaedeutic to a far more important scrutiny. His fundamental criticism concerned the Catholic Church. Socialism, after all, was generated by Roman Catholicism. "French socialism," he writes, "is nothing else but a compulsory communion of mankind—an idea which dates back to ancient Rome and which was fully conserved in Catholicism. Thus, the idea of the liberation of the human spirit from Catholicism became vested there precisely in the narrowest Catholic forms borrowed from the very heart of its spirit, from its letter, from its materialism, from its despotism, from its morality." (*Diary* [January 1877], 2:563.)

In Dostoevsky's view, Roman Catholicism had degenerated to such an extent in Europe that it was directly responsible for the materialism and atheism that was rampant there. Breaking its own association with Christ, even selling Him for earthly rule, the Catholic Church had naturally given birth to the monster of socialism. (*Diary* [November 1877], 2:906.)

Dostoevsky's growing interest in, indeed, preoccupation with, the Catholic Church parallels his deepening concern for religious ideas and value. Just as the thematic route in his novels travels steadily from social, to ethical, philosophical, and finally theological and religious questions, so too, in the last years of his life the "Catholic question" becomes more and more a paramount issue.

In his early writing career, Dostoevsky showed little interest in the Catholic Church. There are only several references to this question in his *Winter Notes*; for instance, where he comments on the "Catholic propaganda" he encountered in England. "As usual," he writes, it was "poking its nose about everywhere, persistent and tireless." (*Winter Notes*, 97.)

Growing Interest in Catholicism

Dostoevsky's interest and criticism intensified graphically, though still on a minor level, while he and his wife remained abroad from 1876 to 1871. Then he became acutely aware of the association between European culture and the Catholic Church. Like Chaadayev, he envisioned Catholicism as the driving force, the essence of Europe. As Zenkovsky had written, "not since Chaadayev was there anyone in Russian literature more conscious of the religious unity than Dostoevsky. That is why he inevitably directs himself to a criticism of Catholicism, the force which has colored all Western culture."[12]

Dostoevsky's hard-nosed critique of Catholicism is first revealed in *The Possessed*. There in the space of one brief paragraph, the trend of his future observations and convictions is laid bare. Europe is described as a den of atheism and socialism because Roman Catholicism had lost all semblance to Christian thought and reality. Dostoevsky uses Shatov and Stavrogin to reveal the shambles remaining of authentic Christianity in Europe.

> But you went further—you believed that Roman Catholicism was no longer Christian. You maintained that Rome had proclaimed a Christ who had succumbed to the Devil's third temptation and that, by announcing to the world that Christ couldn't hold out on earth without an earthly kingdom, Catholicism had really proclaimed the Antichrist and thus was leading the Western world to perdition. You actually said that if France was suffering it was through the fault of Catholicism, because France had rejected the decaying Romish god, but had not found another to replace him. (*The Possessed*, 236.)

Dostoevsky becomes more expansive in the expression of his attitude toward the Catholic Church in his subsequent novel, *The Idiot*. Again the trend of thought is only schematic, compressed into the space of a few pages, the attack breaks through the surface in an explosive outburst of the main character, Myshkin. The incident occurs late in the work in a sudden, almost traumatic manner. In the true Dostoevskian tradition, the dramatic tone is set in an aura of ambiguity and duality.

The outburst of Myshkin, the gentle epileptic, is doubly telling because of the hero's character and the problem of evil he is pitted against. Myshkin is portrayed as a model, even a paragon of virtue. He is something of the grand knight, a Russian Don Quixote who reflects the Christ figure while simultaneously including some features of the "Holy Fool" tradition. Myshkin is the totally selfless person, one who is unable to make negative judgments about other creatures of God. He suspects no one, refuses to throw rocks at his fellow men. In a word, he is the thoroughly "beautiful" person with a heart of gold. These aspects of his character naturally intensify his trenchant critique of Catholicism.

The Idiot *and Russian Apostacy*

While gathered in discussion, Myshkin becomes suddenly agitated with the mention of the name Pavlishtchev. He is described as "positively trembling all over." And then the dialog begins: "Yes, there you have our most excellent and worthy people. Because he was after all a man of family and fortune, a kammerherr, if he had. . . chosen to remain in the service. . . . And then he suddenly threw up the service to go over to the Roman Church and become a Jesuit, and almost openly, with a sort of enthusiasm. It's true, he died in the nick of time . . . everybody said so. . . . (*Idiot*, 531.)

Myshkin is described as being beside himself and interjects: "Pavlishtchev. . . Pavlishtchev, went over to the Roman Church? Impossible!" he cries in horror. Then several members of the discussion banter around the subject of escaping from the wiles of the Jesuits while in Europe. Myshkin is still stunned by the report of the conversion to Catholicism of a man he thought so highly of. "'Pavlishtchev was a clearheaded man and a Christian, a genuine Christian.' Myshkin brought out suddenly. 'How could he have accepted a faith. . . that's unchristian? Catholicism is as good as an unchristian religion!' he added suddenly, looking about him with flashing eyes as though scanning the whole company." (*Idiot*, 532)

At first the participants are taken aback by the rapidity of Myshkin's disclosures. They are not quite sure they have heard correctly, and therefore ask for an explanation. Instead Myshkin delivers a minor lecture on the topic. He repeats Stavrogin's statement that the Catholic Church is devoid of real Christianity. It is noted, moreover, that Myshkin begins his elaboration in "extreme agitation and excessive abruptness." He then distinguishes Catholicism and atheism: "And in the second place Roman Catholicism is even more than atheism itself. In my opinion! Yes, that's my opinion! Atheism only preaches a negation, but Catholicism goes further: it preaches a distorted Christ, a Christ calumniated and defamed by themselves, the opposite of Christ! It preaches the Antichrist, I declare it does, I assure you it does! This is the conviction I have long held, and it has distressed me, myself." (*Idiot*, 532.)

Then to bolster his argument with historical evidence, Myshkin portrays the misguided development of Catholicism in the West, in particular its fateful relationship with the Roman Empire. That is the prime source of Europe's problems that are bringing it to her knees.

> Roman Catholicism cannot hold its position without universal political supremacy, and cries: '*Non Possumus!*' To my thinking Roman Catholicism is not even a religion, but simply the continuation of the Western Roman Empire, and everything in it is subordinated to that idea, faith to begin with. The Pope seized the earth, an earthly throne, and grasped the sword; everything has gone on in the same way since, only they have added to the sword lying, fraud, deceit, fanaticism, superstition, villainy. They have trifled with the most holy, truthful, sincere, fervent feelings of the people; they have bartered it all, all for money, for base earthly power. And isn't that the teaching of Antichrist? How could atheism fail to come from them? Atheism has sprung from Roman Catholicism itself. It originated with them themselves. Can they have believed themselves? It has been strengthened by revulsion from them; it is begotten by their lying and their spiritual impotence! Atheism! Among us it is only the exceptional classes who don't believe, those who, as Yevgeny Pavlovitch splendidly expressed it the other day, have lost their roots. Out over there, in Europe, a terrible mass of the people themselves are beginning to lose their faith—at first from darkness and lying, and now from fanaticism and hatred of the Church and Christianity. (*Idiot*, 532-33.)

Myshkin's fast and furious raking criticism leaves himself breathless and his listeners dumbfounded; one breaks out laughing, another moves closer to the center of the activity with "a spiteful smile on his face." Myshkin attempts to reassure and persuade his listeners of the revelatory nature of his message, retorting that he is speaking of the essence of Roman Catholicism. (*Idiot*, 533.)

When the listeners try to calm Myshkin down, telling him that the whole matter is a theological question, he cuts them short. Indeed, it is a very practical matter of every day significance. It touches them all very closely. Here too the relation of socialism, atheism, and Catholicism is stressed. Atheism and its brother, socialism, are ushered onto the scene because of worn-out Catholic ideas that have paved the way for widespread despair and hatred in the West. Catholicism has failed to "quench the spiritual thirst of parched humanity," and thereby has prepared the avalanche that followed.

Throughout this brief burst of personal conviction Myshkin repeatedly denies the suggestion of his listeners that he has resorted to excessive exaggeration, to an over-ardent expression of his ideas, or to the spirit of lethargy that pervades society. Nor is it because of isolation or excitability. On the contrary, Myshkin counters, it is due to unsatisfied yearnings, from "feverishness, from burning thirst."

True to his creative talent, Dostoevsky then turns what he calls this "wild tirade, this rush of strange and agitated words and confused, enthusiastic ideas," into a dramatic climax centering on the person of Myshkin rather than on his seemingly outlandish ideas. The issue is unresolved when Myshkin creates another scene by knocking over a priceless china vase.

Journalistic Portrayal of Catholicism

The Catholic question continued to haunt Dostoevsky, and with increasing avidity and acceleration, he began to reaffirm and elaborate on his few pithy statements in *The Possessed* and *The Idiot*. Instead of synthesizing in a major novel his contentions and convictions that the Catholic Church had degenerated to a point where it was no longer even Christian, Dostoevsky turned to journalism. *The Diary of a Writer*, a massive collection of 1,052 pages, with issues in 1873, 1876, 1877, August 1880, and January 1881, became his new forum of expression.

In the *Diary* Dostoevsky freely expressed all of his philosophical, political, and theological opinions and convictions. There is virtually no area that he does not touch on, from the subject of courts, cruelty to children, education, international relations, law cases, literature, and wife beating. In December 1876, he set forth the objectives of his *Diary*: "Thus far, the main object of the *Diary* was to explain, as far as possible, the idea of our national spiritual independence, elucidating it in concrete facts as they appear. In this sense, for instance, in the *Diary* there has been considerable discussion of our sudden national and popular movement of this year in connection with the so-called 'Slavic Problem.'" (*Diary* [December 1876], 1:554.)

An important feature of the *Diary* is the bold contrast Dostoevsky establishes between East and West, extolling the great future of Russia in both Europe and Russia. At the same time he writes scathing critiques of the West and the Catholic Church. Indeed, the *Diary* served not only as a forum whereby the author could restate and amplify his earlier views, but more important, it served as a laboratory for his future masterpiece, *The Brothers Karamazov*. In the *Diary* the tone or mood of urgency and prophecy rises to great heights.

Throughout the *Diary*, as we have noted, Dostoevsky makes random remarks on how the West had dimmed the light of Christ and doomed the West to ruin and destruction. He also describes the gradual loss of Christ in history because of the Catholic Church. In his analysis the seeds of corruption were present from the very beginning. When the early communities were formed after Christ, he wrote, the Church almost immediately

> began to seek after its 'civic formula,' fully based upon the moral hope of quenching its spirit in accordance with the principles of individual self-betterment. Christian communes—churches—arose, following which a new, hitherto unheard-of nation began to form itself—all-brotherly, all-humanitarian in the form of an Ecumenical Church. But it was subjected to persecution; its ideal was moulded underground, while on the earth's surface a huge edifice, an enormous ant-hill, was being erected—the ancient Roman Empire, which was also, as it were, an ideal and a solution of the moral aspirations of the ancient world; there arose the demigod, the Empire itself embodied the religious idea providing an outlet to all moral aspirations of the ancient world. The ant hill, however, did not come to pass, having been undermined by the Church. A collision of two diametrically opposed ideas occurred: the man-god encountered the

God-man, Apollo of Belvedere encountered Christ. A compromise took place; the Empire embraced Christianity, while the Church accepted the Roman law and the Roman state. (*Diary* [August 1880], 2:1005.)

According to Dostoevsky, a small part of the Christian Church temporarily escaped the harmful effects of Roman law and retired into the desert and continued the original work of Christ. But then the various branches became estranged to the point where the two major centers of Christianity were cut in half. In the West, the Church was almost totally absorbed by the state. "In the Western part the state, at length, subdued the Church altogether. Meanwhile the East was conquered by the sword of Mohammed, and there remained only Christ detached from the state." (*Diary* [August 1880], 2:1005.)

Old Rome was the first to originate and to attempt to practice the ideal of a universal empire. But the ground plan disintegrated in time, and when the Pax Romana fell, Western Christianity assumed the idea, though not the formula. The old imperial idea gave way to a new ideal, "also universal, of a communion in Christ. This new ideal bifurcated into the Eastern ideal of e purely spiritual communion of men, and the Western European, Roman Catholic, papal ideal diametrically opposite to the Eastern one." (*Diary* [May–June 1877], 2:728.)

Because the papacy subsumed the old ideal of the Roman emperor into a new existence, the West thereby lost its spiritual foundation and at length deteriorated to such an extent "that the Roman papacy proclaimed that Christianity and its idea, without the universal possession of lands and peoples, are not spiritual but political. In other words, that they cannot be achieved without the realization on earth of a new universal Roman empire now headed not by the Roman emperor but by the Pope. And thus it was sought to establish a new universal empire in full accord with the spirit of the ancient Roman world, only in a different form." (*Diary* [May–June 1877], 2:728.)

Roman Law Versus the Eastern Ideal

Dostoevsky contrasted the development of the Orthodox and Catholic churches by stating that in the Eastern ideal the spiritual communion of all in Christ came first; a just state and social communion would naturally result from this unity in Christ. The Roman tradition, he wrote, has an inverse tradition. First a unity was realized through a universal empire; then a spiritual union was achieved, not under Christ, but "under the rule of the Pope as the potentate of this world." (*Diary* [December 1876],) 1:554.)

Dostoevsky constantly—explicitly or implicitly—presented Catholicism as a perverted Christianity which allowed itself to lose its spiritual vigor and forced its adherents to abandon the true faith. Dostoevsky did not dwell on specific, concrete instances in previous world history but merely made these broad generalizations while occupying himself with the flow of events of his own day.

The Crucial Role of France

Like most Russians of his own time, Dostoevsky viewed France as the crucial vortex of events. What happened there provided omens of future trends. More important, France, as the country of old, was thoroughly absorbed in the Catholic idea. Down through the centuries, it had been "as it were, the fullest incarnation of the Catholic idea—the head of this idea which of course was inherited from the Romans and in their spirit." (*Diary* [January 1877], 2:563.) Catholicism, he added, until recent times has been France's "cementing and integral idea." (*Diary* [November 1877], 2:910.)

Above all, Dostoevsky attributed a messianic note to the French nation. As the chief heir of the Roman or Catholic idea, it quite naturally absorbed the primary characteristics that shaped so much of the old world.

> Every great people believes, and must believe if it intends to live long, that in it alone resides the salvation of the world; that it lives in order to stand at the head of nations, to affiliate and unite all of them, and to lead them in a concordant choir toward the final goal preordained for them. When the Catholic idea had been inherited by France the same happened there, and during almost two centuries France, till her most recent debacle and despondency, all the time and undeniably considered herself the mistress of the world at least in the moral domain, and at times also in the political field; the leader of its progress, and the guide of its future. (*Diary* [January 1877], 2:575.)

Dostoevsky viewed the French Revolution of 1789 as a turning point of the religious question in France. For him, the last viable principle of Christianity had been abandoned. France had "lost *virtually all* of her religion (the Jesuits and the atheists there are one and the same)"; several times she closed down the churches and has even "on one occasion subjected God himself to ballot in the Assembly." (*Diary* [January 1877], 2:563.)

The Third Temptation of the Devil

Rome was bound to encounter serious trouble if France fell under the ensuing web of power politics and internal difficulties. If France capitulated, Rome would lose its "sword," its military pressure partner in Europe. The Catholic Church would therefore be forced to initiate a new strategy in order to maintain its hold on the people. And Rome would not give up without a furious fight because it is militant and "will be waging war till the end of the world." (*Diary* [November 1877], 2:910.) Referring to the conspiratorial nature of Roman Catholicism, Dostoevsky declared that

Why, Roman Catholicism is known to have made even sharper turns: once upon a time, when this was necessary, it did not hesitate to sell Christ in exchange for mundane power. Having proclaimed the dogma that "Christianity cannot survive on earth without the earthly power of the Pope," it thereby has proclaimed a new Christ, not like the former one, but one who has been seduced by the third temptation of the devil—the temptation of the kingdoms of the world: 'All these things will I give thee if thou wilt fall down and worship me!' (*Diary* [March 1877], 1:255.)

The Catholic Church does not need Christ, Dostoevsky asserts; its only interest is "universal sovereignty." It will undertake any campaign or strategy to insure its livelihood. "It is inspired with a devilish desire to live, and it is difficult to kill it—it is a snake." (*Diary* [May–June 1877], 2:738.)

Catholicism sold Christ when it blessed the Jesuits and sanctioned the righteousness "of every means for Christ's cause." However, since time immemorial, it has converted Christ's cause into a mere concern for its earthly possessions and its future political domination over the whole world. When Catholic mankind turned away from the monstrous image in which, at length, Christ had been revealed to them—after many protests, reformations, etc., at the beginning of this century—it strove to organize life without God, without Christ. Devoid of the instinct of a bee or an ant, unmistakably and with utmost precision constructing their hive and ant-hill, man sought to create something like an ant-hill. They rejected the unique formula of mankind's salvation, derived from God and announced through revelation to man: "Thou shalt love thy neighbor as thyself," and substituted for it practical inferences, such as "Chacun pour soi et Dieu pour tous" ("Each one for himself and God for all"), or scientific axioms, such as "the struggle for existence." (*Diary* [November 1877], 2:911.)

Roman Socialism

Time and time again Dostoevsky expressed his fear that the Catholic Church's adaptation to the time will entail a merging with or selling out to socialism. He felt that, rather than lose out entirely, the Church would forsake the princes of this world and go to the demos. The representatives of the Church will tell the people that Christ preached the same things as the socialists are now preaching. Once again they will sell Christ as they have "sold Him so many times in the past for earthly possessions, defending the rights of the Inquisition which, in the name of loving Christ, tortured men for freedom of conscience—in the name of Christ to whom only that disciple was dear who came to Him of his free accord and not the one who had been brought or frightened." (*Diary* [November 1877], 2:911.)

Dostoevsky even described the pitiful circumstances in which the Pope of Rome would be compelled to make his appearance to the people: "On foot and barefooted, the Pope will go to all the beggars and he will tell them everything the socialists teach and strive for is contained in the Gospel; that so far the time had not been ripe for them to learn about this; but that now the time has come, and that he, the Pope, surrenders Christ to them and believes in the ant-hill." (*Diary* [May–June 1877], 2:738.)

Pope Pius IX

Dostoevsky's strongest criticism of the Catholic Church in his *Diary* centered on the papacy. He approached this issue, an obvious source of irritation and disgust, from several angles. Aimée Dostoevsky illuminates her father's fascination with the question of the papacy. She says that a Russian writer, a friend of Dostoevsky, could never understand why her father could be so interested in "that old fool the Pope." She adds. "Now to Dostoevsky 'that old fool' was the most interesting figure in Europe."[13]

Arrogance of the Catholic Hierarchy

An equally revealing glimpse into the life experience of Dostoevsky and his relation to the Catholic hierarchy appeared in an early work, *The Gambler.* The scene is a faithful account of an actual episode during Dostoevsky's stay in Europe:

> As I had been certain for the past two days that I might have to go to Rome for a short time on our business, I went to the secretariat of His Holiness's Embassy in Paris to have my passport viséd. There I was met by an abbé, a shrivelled up little man of about fifty, with a frosty face; he heard me out politely, though extremely coldly, and asked me to wait. I was in a hurry, but of course I sat down to wait, took out my *Opinion Nationale* and began reading a dreadful attack on Russia. Meanwhile I heard somebody going through the next room into Monsignore's; I could see my abbé bowing to him. I repeated my former request; even more coldly than before he again asked me to wait. A little later a stranger—some Austrian—came in one business; he was listened to and immediately taken upstairs. Then I got annoyed; I got up, went over to the abbé and told him firmly that as Monsignore was seeing people he could deal with me as well. The abbé positively recoiled in amazement. He simply couldn't understand how an insignificant Russian dared put himself on the same level as Monsignore's guests like that! With the greatest insolence he looked me up and down from head to foot, as though delighted to be able to insult me, and shouted, 'Do you really imagine Monsignore is going to leave his coffee for you?' Then I shouted as well, but louder, 'In that case, let me tell you I don't give a damn for your Monsignore's coffee! If you don't finish with my passport this instant, I shall go to him myself!'
> 'What, when the cardinal is with him?' cried the abbé, recoiling from me in horror, and he rushed to the doors and barred them with outstretched arms, looking as if he would die rather than let me

through. Then I retorted that I was a heretic and a barbarian (que je suis heretique et barbare) and didn't care a straw for his Archbishops and Cardinals and Monsignores, et cetera, et cetera. In short, I didn't look like giving up. The abbé looked at me with unutterable hatred, snatched away my passport and took it upstairs. In one minute it had been viséd. (*The Gambler,* 22–23.)[14]

In the May–June 1877 issue of the *Diary,* Dostoevsky called Pius IX the arch enemy in Europe. He was "leading everybody and everything to whom the Roman idea had been bequeathed," into strife (2:735). "I repeat: in our day the Papacy is, perhaps, the most dreadful among all 'segregations' threatening universal peace." (*Diary* [March 1876], 1:258.) In the unstable and agitated political situation in Europe, Dostoevsky felt, the Catholic Church with the Pope at its head would have the most to gain. Writing in the *Diary* for November 1877, he expressed this conviction. "It stands to reason that slaughter, blood, plunder, even cannibalism would be advantageous to Catholicism. Precisely then it may hope to catch once more its fish in troubled waters, foreseeing the moment when, finally, mankind, exhausted by chaos and lawlessness, will fall into its arms. Then, once more, it will become in reality the sole and absolute 'earthly ruler and universal authority,' sharing its power with no one. Thereby it will attain its ultimate goal." (*Diary* [November 1877], 2:912.)

Kulturkampf

Dostoevsky felt that Bismark alone in Europe understood the real threat behind the papacy. He alone perceived the plight of Europe with a healthy papacy. Therefore he battled with Rome and "persecuted not the Catholic faith but its Roman foundation." (*Diary* [May–June 1877], 2:734.) Here Dostoevsky obviously alluded to Bismark's Kulturkampf and its tactics. Thus Dostoevsky gave moral support to Bismark's endeavor to crush the attempts at a Catholic revival in Europe. The scene focused particularly on the forthcoming death of Pius IX and the election of a new pontiff.

And in Rome it is well known that Prince Bismark is going to use all his power, his best endeavors, to deliver the last and most horrible blow against the papal authority, exercising his utmost influence upon the election of the new Pope so as to convert him—if possible with his own consent—from a secular sovereign and potentate into a Patriarch, and thus, by dividing Catholicism into two rival camps, to bring about once and forever its disintegration and the destruction of its claims and hopes. (*Diary* [September 1877], 2:825.)

Papal Infallibility

Dostoevsky noted the insistence with which Pius IX stared danger in the face, notably on the occasion of Vatican I when he boldly proclaimed the doctrine of infallibility. It was then that Pius finally revealed "the whole secret," as Dostoevsky puts it, about the Church. The Pope took this resolute stand precisely when a united Italy was clamoring at the gates of Rome itself. The Pope, then, was by no means a weak man as many thought; indeed, he was prepared to fight to the death for the life of the Church.

The "secret" Dostoevsky refers to is the allegedly everlasting thrust for power on the part of the papacy, a theme Dostoevsky repeats on numerous occasions, This, he felt, was made abundantly clear at Vatican I:

> But there always has been a secret: during many centuries the Popes have been pretending that they were satisfied with their tiny dominion—the Papal State; but all this was for the sake of mere allegory; still, the important point is that in this allegory there was always hidden the kernel of the main idea, coupled with the indubitable and perpetual hope of papacy in the future the kernel would grow into a grand tree which would shade the whole world. (*Diary* [March 1876], 1:255–56.)

Dostoevsky depicted the events preceding the declaration of infallibility as one of hostility and defeat. Yet, as if getting up from his death bed, Pius announced to the world, "urbi et orbi" the real state of the question:

> So you thought that I was satisfied with the mere title of King of the Papal State? Know that I have ever considered myself potentate of the whole world and over all earthly kings, and not only their spiritual, but their mundane, genuine master sovereign and emperor. It is I who am king over all kings and sovereign over all sovereigns, and to me alone on earth belong the destinies, the ages and the bounds of time. And now I am proclaiming this in the dogma of my infallibility. (*Diary* [March 1876], 1:256.)

For Dostoevsky this triumphant declaration was merely a belated confession, a mere resurrection and repetition of the old Roman imperial idea, and it marked the complete sale of Christ for the kingdoms of this world. Faith in God had been at once replaced by faith in the Pope. In the process, the vertical or transcendental element of religion and the spiritual life had been exterminated to assure temporarily the survival of the Church.

Dostoevsky frequently contrasted his view of the Roman Church and the papacy with that of the liberals' of his era. In this respect he described a Roman Church filled with an insatiable desire to live, willing to use any strategy, even conspiracy, to achieve its goals. The liberals, on the other hand, were unrealistic in their view of what was taking place in Europe. This is clear in his imaginative picture of the Pope reduced to his last impotent state:

> Oh, isn't it true that this would sound funny and insignificant to politicians and diplomats of Europe! The downtrodden Pope, imprisoned in the Vatican, appeared to them during the last years as such a nullity that it would have been a shame to pay any attention to him. Thus many progressives of Europe have been reasoning, especially the witty and liberal ones, The pope delivering allocutions and issuing syllabuses, receiving devotionalists, damning and dying—in their view resembled a buffoon performing for their entertainment. The thought that an enormous universal idea which had been conceived in the brain of the devil when he was tempting Christ in the wilderness; an idea which has been organically living in the world one thousand years; that this idea, nevertheless would die in an instant—was taken for granted. (*Diary* [May–June 1877], 2:736.)

The narrator of *The Possessed* had a similar view. "We also frequently drifted into matters concerning mankind as a whole, discussing the future of Europe and the fate of man, forecasting dogmatically that Caesarism would reduce France to a second-rate power, a thing we were certain was imminent. The pope, we felt sure, would become just another cardinal in a unified Italy, and there wasn't the slightest doubt in our minds that this thousand-year-old matter would be settled with a snap of the fingers in our age of humanitarianism, industry, and railroads." (*The Possessed*, 35.)

Papal Barbarism in the Russo-Turkish War

Dostoevsky especially accused Rome and the papacy during the brief flareup on the Eastern Question, the Russo-Turkish War of 1877–78. Dostoevsky made this struggle the heart of his comments in the *Diary* at this time. There in the south, he writes, thousands of Christians are being exterminated like bugs and reptiles, "in the presence of their mothers, infants are being thrown up into the air to be caught on rifle-bayonets; villages are being annihilated; churches smashed into splinters; everything, without exception is being *exterminated*—and this by a savage, disgusting Mohammedan horde, the sworn enemy of civilization." (*Diary* [July–August 1876], 1:376.)

The West, militant Catholicism at the forefront, chose to back Turkey in this battle against "schismatic Russia." To Dostoevsky this was significant proof, once more, of the intrigues and conspiracy behind the Roman idea. He was particularly appalled at the pope's expression of satisfaction and joy at Russian reverses. This was proof positive of papal hatred for Russia.

> Not some prelate, but the pope himself, loudly and with joy, spoke at the Vatican Conferences about 'the victories of the Turks prophesying to Russia a dreadful future.' This dying old man, and besides—'the head of Christianity,' was not ashamed to announce *urbi et orbi* that every time he hears with joy about Russian reverses. This awful hatred becomes quite intelligible if it is admitted that at present Catholicism is actually 'militating' and that, by deed, i.e , *with the sword*, it is waging a war in Europe against its dreaded and fatal enemies. (*Diary* [September 1877], 2:823.)

Dostoevsky referred to the stance of Pius on the Turkish question as one of "bestiality," and "barbarism," stating that the Pope prayed for the "torturers of Christianity," hoping they would vanquish the Russians who rose up in Christ's name for the defense of Christianity. (*Diary* [May–June 1877], 2:696.)[15]

Nevertheless, Dostoevsky felt that the Eastern question would eventually backfire on militant Catholicism and result in an European blood bath where centuries' old questions would be resolved in a way totally unfavorable to Rome and the papacy. In the long run, therefore, there was nothing to fear from the campaign in the south, because Catholicism was perhaps enjoying its last dying gasp in the West.

Final Synthesis on Catholicism

While continuing to express his opinions and convictions on the great issues of the day in 1878, Dostoevsky began making more and more time available for an endeavor he had long looked forward to, his fifth major novel. With the publication of *A Raw Youth* in 1875 Dostoevsky had given himself sufficient time to mull over his new ideas and synthesize a new approach to the religious question.

As far back as 1868, Dostoevsky had planned a book to be entitled "The Life of a Great Sinner." In this project he intended to draw up a sweeping comparison between Catholicism and Jesuitry, and Orthodoxy. The chief idea of the work, he writes, "is one that has tormented me, consciously and unconsciously, all my life long: it is the question of the existence of God. (*Letters*, 159, 190.)[16] Along with the material accumulated during the laboratory period of the *Diary*, Dostoevsky used these ideas as the moulding force of his last novel. By 1879 his work began to appear serially in the *Russkiy Vestnik* and in 1880 in book form.

Thematic of The Brothers Karamazov

As Dostoevsky had planned years before, *The Brothers Karamazov* pitted faith versus atheism. Dmitry says in the novel, "The awful thing is that beauty is mysterious as well as terrible. God and the devil are fighting there and the battlefield is the heart of men." (*Brothers Karamazov*, 127.) Could spiritual forces would overcome the materialistic elements of the world? The question was whether "with an hereditary sensualism, good could triumph over evil, the evil of thought as well as of deed, and form out of the very tendency a source of strength to combat the weakness and wickedness inherent in human beings."[17]

The Brothers Karamazov *as Peak of Dostoevsky's Writing*

Most critics agree that Dostoevsky reached the pinnacle of his creative prose mastery with *The Brothers Karamazov*. But there is one notable exception: "I feel that, in one sense, Dostoevsky had passed his zenith when he came to write it and that, though his mind remained as alert as ever, his creative capacity, as almost always happens with an ageing novelist, had begun to wane. . . . it carries, despite its enormous energy, the mark of a tired brain.[18]

Freud in contrast, placed Dostoevsky just behind Shakespeare. "*The Brothers Karamazov* is the most magnificent novel ever written; the episode of the Grand Inquisitor, one of the peaks in the literature of the world, can hardly be valued too highly. Before the problem of the creative artist analysis must, alas, lay down its arms."[19]

The most striking and compelling part of *The Brothers Karamazov* is unquestionably "The Grand Inquisitor." In the space of some twenty pages Dostoevsky surpasses the reaches of his previous creative artistry. Of the mass of startling and provocative ideas that Dostoevsky offers to his readers, the little "poem" that Ivan recites, has evoked the greatest variety of questions and interpretations. Each section of this study has pointed toward understanding this product of a "cruel talent."

Problem of Unity of Book

Here it is crucial to recall the setting and motivation of "The Grand Inquisitor." Guardini, in his perceptive article, believes that the episode is not detachable from the novel, that it cannot be properly understood apart from the entire novel. "The habit of considering it as a detachable section falsifies the spiritual intention of the work and destroys the artistic welding of its various parts, giving even the whole some painful appearance of demagogic special pleading."[20]

Kesich makes the same point. "This story of Ivan's is not isolated and cannot be discussed without reference to the book as a whole. The Legend is inseparably linked to the events that precede it, as well as to those that follow it. The dominant note of the whole book is given in this story."[21]

Curle takes a counter position. In his view, the episode is "complete in itself, and, if omitted from the novel, would not affect it in the slightest.[22]

We share Curle's view, which is confirmed by information provided in Rahv's study. In 1902 one witness, V. F. Putzikovich, published an account of a conversation he had had with the novelist in the summer of 1879, while *The Brothers Karamazov* was still running serially in the *Russkiy Vestnik*. Dostoevsky called the chapter on the Grand Inquisitor the culminating point of his creative career. When questioned on his reasons for interpolating a devised legend of sixteenth-century Spain into a narrative of contemporary Russia, he answered that its theme had haunted him since early youth; for fear that he might not live to finish another major work, he had resolved to try his hand at it without delay and to incorporate it in the novel he was then writing.[23]

This difference of opinion is no mere quibble. It grounds the correct interpretation of the Grand Inquisitor episode.

There is almost unanimous agreement about the central thrust of the Grand Inquisitor. Berdyayev states that this episode "may be interpreted chiefly as directed against Roman Catholicism and revolutionary socialism. But in actual fact the subject is broader and deeper. It is the theme of the kingdom of Caesar, of the rejection of the temptation of the Kingdoms of this world." Moreover, "In actual fact *The Legend of The Grand Inquisitor* strikes a terrible blow at all authority and all power, it lashes out at the kingdom of Caesar not only in Roman Catholicism but also in Orthodoxy and in every religion, just as in communism and socialism."[24]

Kesich adopts the position of Berdyayev though his rationale may not be as sound as it seems at first glimpse.

> On the surface the Legend appears to be an attack on Roman Catholicism. . . . The meaning of the Legend is not revealed if it is regarded primarily as an attack on the Roman Catholic Church. Apart from the chapter in which the Legend is found, *The Brothers Karamazov* does not deal with the Roman Church, yet the novel is intimately related to the Legend. The Legend is concerned with Russia, not with Rome. It is written mainly to confront the Christ of the New Testament with a radical atheistic humanist.[25]

Object of Dostoevsky's Attack

Sandoz in his comprehensive study of the question agrees on the general thrust of Dostoevsky's critique: "The savage caricature of institutionalized Christianity given there cannot be read as only an attack on Roman Catholicism. It is likewise a pitiless condemnation of the

Caesaropapism of Russian Orthodoxy and the hierarchy of the Church for succumbing to Satan's temptations and accepting the paltry reward of earthly domination at the expense of spiritual bread."[26]

Guardini follows the logic of Berdyayev and Kesich, stating that "it is the Roman Church and especially her hierarchy which is being aimed at here, but above all, as the most resolute expression of her spirit, the Jesuit order." Guardini then softens the blow of the critique: "But the ensemble of the novel shows clearly that this obvious and banal interpretation of the legend cannot be its true meaning, because the Church does not play any role in the book."[27] If examined rightly, he adds, "we will quickly perceive that the criticism of Rome cannot in any way constitute the essence of the 'Grand Inquisitor,' and moreover, that we would be doing Dostoevsky himself a real disservice to interpret the legend in this unilateral way. For controversy has not only been Dostoevsky's weakest side, but also his least admirable."[28]

Mokulsky maintains a similar interpretation. "Dostoevsky thought that in *The Legend* he was unmasking Catholicism's deception and the lie of socialism; but his exposure went further and deeper."[29]

Guardini and Kesich substantiate their positions, in part by the supposedly logical notion of coherence of the entire work of *The Brothers Karamazov*. However, this is a patently weak method and is by no means borne out in the other works of Dostoevsky; in *The Possessed*, *The Idiot*, and *A Raw Youth*, Dostoevsky cannot always be verified on the strictly logical plane.

The Legend: *Attack on Catholicism*

What Dostoevsky does, and this is obvious in all his published material, is to maintain a consistent, immovable view of the Catholic Church. He follows a persistent pattern throughout his literary career in this regard and the insistence of his critique grows with the years. Clearly, the burden of Dostoevsky's sharp criticism of the Catholic Church should not be underemphasized or downgraded as Berdyayev, Guardini, Kesich, Mokulsky and Sandoz suggest, even though their own interpretations may be motivated by the spirit of balance itself.

Admittedly, this a question of degree. Zenkovsky has a more accurate appraisal of the purpose and scope of the Grand Inquisitor: "Dostoevsky purposely chose the form of a legend to express his most concentrated and incisive criticism of the Catholic idea, which he considers to be the basis of European culture. What is important for him is the true meaning of the spirit and idea of Catholicism, rather than its individual expressions or exact formulas."[30]

As in his previous novels, letters, and *Diary*, so too in his last creative work, Dostoevsky aimed his barbs at the Catholic Church. In these other works also, the space allotted to the Catholic idea is minimal and the treatment is sporadic. Dostoevsky is quite consistent.

Dostoevsky began his attack on the Catholic Church early in *The Brothers Karamazov*. The argument is has two aspects, positive and negative, which both are long standing concerns of Dostoevsky. From one side the discussion involves some "new" ideas on the jurisdiction of the church and what the implications bring to bear on the old distinction between Church and State. In depicting Ivan's novel views, Dostoevsky avails himself of the opportunity, from the other side, of expressing his general opposition to the "Catholic idea."

Ivan's Article

Ivan's article suggests that the Church ought to include the entire State and "not simply to occupy a corner in it, and, if this is, for some reason, impossible at present, then it ought, in reality, to be set up as the direct and chief aim of the future development of Christian society. (*Brothers Karamazov*, 68–69.) Miüsov, "impatiently crossing and recrossing his legs" cries out, "the purest Ultramontanism!" (*Brothers Karamazov*, 69.) Ivan's reiteration that the state should be transformed into the Church naturally evokes a comparison of Church-State relationships in the West. This, in turn, allows the Elder Zossima to comment that "in many cases there are no churches there at all, for though ecclesiastics and splendid church buildings remain, the churches themselves have long ago striven to pass from Church into State and to disappear in it completely. So it seems at least in Lutheran countries. As for Rome, it was proclaimed a State instead of a Church a thousand years ago." (*Brothers Karamazov*, 73–74.)

As the discussion draws to its close, Miüsov becomes completely aghast at the trend of the remarks, dumbfounded at the conclusions reached by his companions. "Why, it's beyond anything! . . . The State is eliminated and the Church is raised to the position of the State. It's not simply Ultramontanism, it's archultramontanism! It's beyond the dreams of Pope Gregory the Seventh!" (*Brothers Karamazov*, 75.) Then Father Païssy, the "learned monk," makes another thrust for Dostoevsky against Rome:

> You are completely misunderstanding it. . . . understand the Church is not to be transformed into the State. That is Rome and its dream. That is the third temptation of the devil. On the contrary, the State is transformed into the Church, will ascend and become a Church over the whole world—which is the complete opposite of Ultramontanism and Rome, and your interpretation, and is only the glorious destiny ordained for the Orthodox Church. (*Brothers Karamazov*, 75.)

The dialog centering around Ivan's article gives Dostoevsky another opportunity to recapitulate his views on the Catholic Church. It also assumes a warming-up or prelude to his most devastating critique of the Catholic idea in the Grand Inquisitor. This is an interesting artifice on Dostoevsky's part, using the brilliance and penetration of a man who is supposedly swayed only by cold logic. Now obliquely, now at point-blank range, it is he who holds forth on the question of Church-State relationships and the Catholic idea.

In a letter of May 10, 1879, to N. A. Liubimov, associate editor of *Russky Vestnik*, Dostoevsky reveals an important insight into the character portrayal of Ivan, which is crucial for a correct understanding of the major features of the Grand Inquisitor.

> In the copy I've just sent you, I describe only the character of one of the leading figures of the novel, one who expresses his basic convictions. These convictions are what I consider the *synthesis* of contemporary Russian anarchism. The denial not of God, but of the meaning of his creation. The whole of socialism sprang up and started with the denial of the meaning of historical actuality, and arrived at the program of destruction and anarchism. The principal anarchists were, in many cases, sincerely convinced men. My hero takes a theme, in my view, an unassailable one: the senselessness of the suffering of children, and from it deduces the absurdity of the whole of historical actuality. (*Pis'ma* 4:53.)

Identification of Characters with Dostoevsky

There are a host of opinions on the proper identification of the characters of Ivan, Christ, and the Inquisitor with Dostoevsky. D. H. Lawrence says, "If there is any question: Who is the Grand Inquisitor?—then surely we must say it is Ivan himself."[31] Curle writes that "Dostoevsky was more interested in ideas than in characters—at least, more able to express ideas than to create characters—and many of his profoundest and loftiest musings were put into Ivan's mouth. . . . It is too obviously Dostoevsky speaking through his mouthpiece."[32]

Guardini says that "Ivan himself is the Grand Inquisitor in so far as he rejects the world and wishes to tear it from the hands of God, since he has made it badly, with the pretension of organizing it differently and in a superior manner than its original author."[33]

Rahv in perhaps one of the deepest insights on the Legend states that

> the Legend as a whole, in its interplay of drama and ideology, is to be taken, I think, as an experiment, one of those experiments in frightfulness with which modern literature has the deepest affinity. Dostoevsky stands at two removes from the Inquisitor, and Ivan at one remove; and this placing or aesthetic 'distancing,' reflects precisely the degree of commitment we are entitled to assume. Therefore to identify Ivan wholly with the Inquisitor, as so many commentators have done, is an error, though a lesser one than that of wholly identifying Dostoevsky with him. The fact is that the Legend has not one but two protagonists, Jesus and the Inquisitor, and that Ivan makes no real choice between them. Jesus is freedom and transcendent truth, whereas the Inquisitor typifies the implacable logic of historical reality; but so stark a confrontation in itself demonstrates that Ivan's dilemma is absolute. After all, he has no God to whom he can appeal for a guaranty of his choice; Jesus is his hero but not his God. Ivan, like his creator, is split through and through, torn between love and contempt, pride and submission, reason and faith, teleology and the extremest pessimism."[34]

Placement of The Legend

Before the actual episode of the Grand Inquisitor, Dostoevsky cleverly manipulates the psychological dilemma of Ivan's alleged inability to accept the problem of evil in this world, notably the suffering of innocents. Here Dostoevsky marshals forth the most debased cruelty of man to helpless children. He depicts "artistically cruel" adults in action: Turks blowing out the brains of a baby, a general setting his dogs on a young boy, tearing him to pieces before his mother's eyes, parents beating unmercifully their five-year-old daughter and locking her up in a frozen privy after they smear her with human excrement. This account of suffering innocents is shrewdly calculated to make the episode of the Grand Inquisitor all the more soul-searching under the glimpse of Ivan.

From the problem of innocent suffering, Ivan leaps into the problem of global suffering, all mankind. First he focuses on a small cross section, those heretics in Seville during "the most terrible time of the Inquisition, when fires were lighted every day to the glory of God." (*Brothers Karamazov*, 295.)

Appearance of Jesus

In this incredible scene, Jesus Christ makes a second appearance on earth where just a day previously heretics were burned to death "in the presence of the king, the court, the knights, the cardinals, the most charming ladies of the court, and the whole population of Seville." (*Brothers Karamazov*, 295.) In effect Ivan has successfully transposed his theme of inhuman suffering from little children to adults. The guilt, moreover, now rests with the Catholic Church, not with some unknown parents or adults.

Ivan paints a compelling contrast between Christ and the Grand Inquisitor. Jesus, except for the two words, "Maiden, arise!", is absolutely silent throughout the interlude. He is passive and submissive to all that takes place there in Seville. The old man of ninety, tall and erect with his withered face and sunken eyes, on the other hand, is in complete control of the entire city. He has, in effect, condemned Jesus to silence.

Excursus on the Jesuits

Jesus has come to "hinder" the work of his followers, but the Grand Inquisitor will not allow any change in the strategy. As Ivan points out to Alyosha, Jesus doesn't have the right "to add anything to what

He has said of old." (*Brothers Karamazov*, 297.) Ivan then proceeds to make one of his most telling blows: "One may say it is the most fundamental feature of Roman Catholicism, in my opinion at least. 'All has been given by Thee to the Pope,' they say, 'and all, therefore, is still in the Pope's hands, and there is no need for Thee to come now at all. Thou must not meddle for the time, at least.' That's how they speak and write too—the Jesuits, at any rate. I have read it myself in the works of their theologians." (*Brothers Karamazov*, 297.)

It is important to pause here, however briefly, to highlight Dostoevsky's personal convictions concerning the Jesuits. The author had more than a passing interest in the "Pope's army." Indeed, Dostoevsky's entire corpus of articles and novels is dotted with sarcasm, satire, and vituperation toward the Society of Jesus. There are no benign words in his quiver for this branch of the Catholic Church. In the *Diary* for January 1877, for instance, Dostoevsky states that in France "the Jesuits and atheists there are one and the same." In *The Idiot* Myshkin refers to "atheism," "Jesuitism," and "nihilism" in the same breath. In the *Diary* for November 1877 he associated the Jesuits with the philosophy and program "of every means for Christ's cause." The Jesuits, then, are plotters *par excellence*, notable for their casuistry, cunning, and conspiratorial nature.

Dostoevsky was especially embittered, as earlier indicated, when native Russians became unpatriotic enough to defect to the West. But when any individual went one step further and joined the Catholic Church, he was doubly troubled. In *Winter Notes*, 76, Dostoevsky obliquely refers to such an individual. The incident that angered him the most involved Prince Ivan Gagarin who left Russia in 1843. He made his home in France, converted to the Catholic Church, and later joined the Society of Jesus. This made a lasting impression on Dostoevsky, and in the *Diary* for June 1876 he recalls with chagrin that "the full-blooded, ancient Prince Gagarin, having become a European, deemed it necessary not only to embrace Catholicism but straightway to leap over to the Jesuits." The same theme is repeated during Myshkin's attack on the Catholic Church (*Idiot*, 531).

All of Dostoevsky's thrusts at the Jesuits pale in comparison with his repeated return to this question in *The Brothers Karamazov*. The Jesuits are always involved in derisive contexts. Even Ivan's "visitor" is allowed his parting shot, reveling in the fact that "those Jesuit confessionals are really my most delightful diversion at melancholy moments." (*Brothers Karamazov*, 786.) But the great novelist saved his most biting acid for the episode of the Grand Inquisitor, where the world has been handed over into the power of Jesuitical Rome.

Because of this commentary on the Jesuits, Fülöp-Miller calls Dostoevsky "the greatest enemy of the Society of Jesus that had arisen since Pascal."[35] In some groundwork sketches of the Grand Inquisitor, Dostoevsky comments on Jesuit Catholicism. "The mind which distorts Christianity by bringing it into harmony with the aims of this world destroys the whole meaning of Christianity. Instead of the high ideal which Christ set up, we have a second Tower of Babel, and, under the banner of love for humanity, contempt for humanity appears undisguised."[36] As Fülöp-Miller points out, Dostoevsky was fully aware that no Jesuit ever held the office of Grand Inquisitor in Spain, who, indeed, is called and dressed as a monk; "nevertheless, he endowed the figure of this spiritual judge, who in Ivan Karamazov's legend has to justify himself to the returned Savior, with the characteristic features of a Jesuit, for the novelist regarded the fathers of the Society of Jesus as the most important representatives of the Catholic spirit, the men who by their worldly wisdom, their skill in dialectic and their ethical system were the first to furnish the Catholic aspirations after power with spiritual weapons."[37]

Confrontation of Inquisitor and Jesus

As the scene unfolds, the old man tells Jesus that the masses have willingly sold their freedom, yet the people believe that they live in perfect freedom. Did not Christ give his early followers the right to bind and unbind? (Mt 16:19) Now freedom has vanished. "For fifteen centuries we have been wrestling with Thy freedom, but now it is ended and over for good." (*Brothers Karamazov*, 298.)

The chief argument of the old man against Christ is that man has been created, endowed, and overburdened with too much freedom. Christ has loaded man down to such an extent that freedom has become a curse instead of a blessing. Spiritual bread, moreover, is not enough for man to live on. Christ has neglected to "feed" man. But the Catholic Church has taken up the slack here.

Bread from Stones: Socialism

In the account of the stones being changed into bread, Dostoevsky subtly raises the question of socialism and the Church again. Socialism, as seen in the *Diary*, is offered as a panacea for man's unhappiness. Rahv has caught the significance of Dostoevsky's suggestive commentary.

> What is first to be accounted for is the strange amalgam of socialism and Catholicism. The critique of socialism is no more than insinuated in the Legend. Its specifications of time and place are such that socialism can come into it only through oblique references and allusions of an allegoric nature. Thus in the Inquisitor's gloss on the Gospel story of 'the temptation,' the motif of 'stones turned into bread' is brought in again and again so as to convert it into the formula for socialism. The linkage of socialism with the Roman Church, though it may strike western readers as fantastic, is integral to Dostoevsky's thought.[38]

Human Happiness and Deception

The Grand Inquisitor reveals to Christ that the leaders of the Church have prepared themselves to do anything to make the people happy, even to deceive them if necessary. As he says, "They will marvel at us and look on us as gods, because we are ready to endure the freedom which they have found so dreadful and to rule them—so awful it will seem to them to be free. But we shall tell them that we are Thy servants and rule them in Thy name. We shall deceive them again, for we will not let Thee come to us again." (*Brothers Karamazov*, 301.)

The Triple Temptation of Jesus

The Inquisitor points out that the very things which Jesus rejected have become the cornerstone of the new people of God. The triple temptation of the Devil: miracle, mystery, and authority are the three greatest needs of the people. "There are three powers, three powers alone, able to conquer and to hold captive forever the conscience of these impotent rebels for their happiness—those forces are miracle, mystery and authority." (*Brothers Karamazov*, 303.)

Since Christ rejected the very things that his people long for the most, the Inquisitor states that his men have taken over for the sake of the people. "We have corrected Thy work and have founded it upon *miracle, mystery* and *authority*. And men rejoiced that they were again led like sheep, and that the terrible gift that had brought them such suffering, was, at last, lifted from their hearts." (*Brothers Karamazov*, 305.)

The Secret of the Inquisitor

At last the Inquisitor reveals his own terrible secret to Jesus. Jesus has been abandoned altogether. It is not so much a question of "correcting" His work, but of giving allegiance to an alien power.

> We are not working with Thee, but with *him*—that is our mystery. It's long—eight centuries—since we have been on *his* side and not on Thine. Just eight centuries ago, we took from him what Thou didst reject with scorn, that last gift he offered Thee, showing Thee all the kingdoms of the earth. We took from him Rome and the sword of Caesar, and proclaimed ourselves sole rulers of the earth, though hitherto we have not been able to complete our work. O, the work is only beginning, but it has begun. It has long to await completion and the earth has yet much to suffer, but we shall triumph and shall be Caesars, and then we shall plan the universal happiness of man. But Thou mightest have taken even then the sword of Caesar. Why didst Thou reject that last gift? Hadst Thou accepted that last counsel of the mighty spirit, Thou wouldst have accomplished all that man seeks on earth—that is, some one to worship, some one to keep his conscience, and some means of uniting all in one unanimous and harmonious ant-heap, for the craving for universal unity is the third and last anguish of men. Mankind as a whole has always striven to organize a universal state. . . . For who can rule men if not he who holds their conscience and their bread in his hands? We have taken the sword of Caesar, and in taking it, of course, have rejected Thee and followed *him*. (*Brothers Karamazov*, 305-6.)

Wasiolek has an interesting comment:

> The Grand Inquisitor's argument is not based on idle rhetoric or cheap tricks. Nor is it contradictory as some have claimed. Logic is on his side, not Christ's, although the truth of each is finally subject

to more than logic. Lawrence, Shestov, Guardini, Rozanov, and many other distinguished critics have taken the side of the Grand Inquisitor against Christ because his argument is powerful and indeed unanswerable. And they do this despite the fact that Dostoevsky made the case he wanted to make for Christ. There is no weakness in Christ's argument, and there is no weakness in the Grand Inquisitor's argument. Mochulsky's argument that the Grand Inquisitor is wrong because he argues from love of mankind, yet portrays mankind as weak and slavish is clearly a *non sequitur*.[39]

The Donation of Pepin

Dostoevsky here is undoubtedly suggesting, as far as the time element is concerned, that the Catholic Church sold out in the eighth century during the "donation of Pepin" in 756 and the rise of papal supremacy over the Church. Included in this era and later would be the slow, imperceptible rift between western and eastern Christianity.

Alyosha's Defence

As Ivan comes to a pause after relating that the Inquisitor threatens to burn the real Christ alive, Alyosha rushes into the fray in a wild flurry of words. He defends the Orthodox Church and makes a token defense of the Catholic Church, but his words actually underscore the alleged reality. By Alyosha's insistence that the Jesuits are not as bad as they seem, as bad as Ivan portrays them, Dostoevsky can give more punch to his unveiling of the inner core of the Jesuits and the Catholic Church.

> That's not the idea of it in the Orthodox Church. . . . That's Rome, and not even the whole of Rome, it's false—those are the worst kind of Catholics, the Inquisitors, the Jesuits! . . . We know the Jesuits, they are spoken ill of, but surely they are not what you describe? They are not that at all, not at all. . . . They are simply the Romish army for the earthly sovereignty of the world in the future, with the Pontiff of Rome for Emperor. . . that's their ideal, but there's no sort of mystery or lofty melancholy about it. . . . It's simple lust of power, of filthy earthly gain, of domination—something like a universal serfdom with them as masters—that's all they stand for. They don't even believe in God perhaps. (*Brothers Karamazov*, 309.)

When Alyosha surmises that the Inquisitor does not even believe in God, Ivan confirms his guess. In effect the Catholic Church, in the person of the Inquisitor, no longer preserves the spiritual content of Jesus Christ. What remains is only a facade, an exterior form to maintain appearances. Ivan further suggests that it requires only one leading figure of the Church to perpetrate such a travesty in religious history. "More than that, one such standing at the head is enough to create the actual leading idea of the Roman Church with all its armies and Jesuits, its highest idea. I tell you frankly that I firmly believe that there has always been such a man among those who stood at the head of the movement. Who knows, there may have been some such even among the Roman Popes." (*Brothers Karamazov*, 311.)

The episode of the Grand Inquisitor closes Dostoevsky's sweeping critique of Roman Catholicism. In it he reached the heights of his creative mastery and struck with the utmost force at what he considered the heart of the Catholic idea. In essence the symbolic content of the story represents the breakdown and corruption of Rome. In the process the Inquisitor's spirit, more specifically the Antichrist, had replaced Christ in the West.

Critique of Ecclesiasticism

The focus of Dostoevsky's critique is clearly the all-pervasive role of ecclesiasticism. This concept summarises the burden of his attention. As Lossky has written in his interpretive study, ecclesiasticism replaced actual, living communication with God. Left in the traces wasa system of guarantees of salvation through various formulae, practices, and rituals.[40]

Conclusion: Dichotomy of East and West

In abstract terms, and here we are dealing with a difference of emphasis in western and eastern philosophy and theology, Dostoevsky suggests that there was far too little of the concept and reality of Christian immanence in the West. In other words, the West has imprisoned Christ and replaced him with authority, papacy, and the Jesuits. The stress on a transcendental Christ isolated man from his own Creator.

Instead of having a living Christ in the Church's body, there was only a wall of external unity which replaced liberty in an atmosphere marked with compromise, compulsion, and expediency. Dostoevsky's insistence, moreover, that the Church of the West was locked on a path taking it further and further away from the pristine faith of early Christianity could not be put more painfully than Ivan's closing remark to Alyosha: "Surely you don't suppose I am going straight off to the Jesuits, to join the men who are correcting His work?" (*Brothers Karamazov*, 312.)

CONCLUSION

No country or period had writers and thinkers as obsessed with the destiny and the historical mission of their nations as nineteenth century Russia.[1] Indeed,

> Russian thought has been tortured for the last century with the overwhelming desire to solve the problem of its own existence. Perhaps no other nation has ever set itself with such burning real to analyse and define its hopes and aspirations, its fears and failures, in the effort to drive to its last refuge the mysterious problem of culture and nationality. For nearly a millennium Russia has experienced either a frenzied struggle to plunge itself into the European sea or an equally fanatical attempt to isolate itself from all that reminds it of the accursed West. On the other hand, the followers of Peter the Great sought to lose their national customs and almost their cultural existence, to become European in the fullest sense of the word. On the other hand, mediaeval and Muscovite Russia and its descendants to this day have seen in the regions to the West the kingdom of Antichrist, the land where virtue is absent and where faith is lost.[2]

Our study has shown that Dostoevsky occupied the bulk of his working days in wrestling with this issue. Indeed, few writers of his day felt so compelling a desire, one might say vocation, to solve the cosmic problems of nineteenth-century Russia. He felt chosen to fulfill this task. Dostoevsky considered himself a national prophet, and was hailed as such by his contemporaries. His journalism was as an important part of this mission to teach his nation and speak for it as his novels.[3] For many reasons, such as the absence of free political life, the Russian novel became a depository of social, political, moral, and religious ideas, more than anywhere else in the modern world. This situation placed the writer in a position of great responsibility. The readers looked on him as a teacher of life; he felt obliged to answer their expectations.[4]

As a leading Russian spokesman of his era, Dostoevsky was quite naturally deeply embedded in the Russian tradition, absorbed in the historical continuity and flow of events. Since his country was the spiritual heir of Byzantium, he too became automatically absorbed in the polemical traditions entrenched throughout Europe and Russia over the centuries.

Russia's relations with the West, as we have seen, would have been far different had not Vladimir's Rus' adopted Orthodoxy from Constantinople rather than the Christianity of Rome and the West. As a result, patterns of life between East and West developed differently in philosophy, religious practice, and theology. All of these qualified Russian politics and culture. This point is borne out, for instance, by the incident of the Raskol in the mid-seventeenth century.

As evidenced by the failures of the Florentine Union, of the Brest Union of 1595-96, and of other attempts to bridge the gaps between East and West, the two sides became hopelessly divided. Russian wars against any Western country became holy wars against the servants of the Devil. This role of apocalyptic struggle especially characterizes the relationship of Moscow to Poland and Rome from the mid-sixteenth century through much of the seventeenth century.

During the Polish-Russian debacles, the Jesuits earned their reputation as dangerous liars, schemers, and treacherous individuals. In the eyes of the Russians, the Poles, led by the Jesuits, symbolized the Catholic conspiracy to defile Orthodox Russia. This symbol survived unmythologized into the nineteenth century to Dostoevsky's day. Despite the efforts of Peter the Great, East and West found their estrangement in their own *oikumene* inescapable, wrapped up in their own spiritual iron curtains.

Dostoevsky battled mightily with the Western Question throughout his life. Acutely conscious of the patterns inherited from the centuries before, he strove to elevate the Russian sense of achievement and national destiny in his countrymen. Russia, he felt, need not fear any comparison with the West. Dostoevsky's "messianic feeling arose . . . from a patriotic rejection of the assumption of the unchanging backwardness of Russia, of its inferiority to the West."[5]

For Dostoevsky, religion was Russia's special prerogative. As our study indicates, he had to settle this question first on a personal basis, and later on a national level. Dwelling on the riddle of the mystery of man, Dostoevsky was led to the only beautiful person in existence, Jesus Christ. For him, Russia more than any other country was most closely associated with the message and teachings of this Christ. Christianity, Orthodoxy, the Russian people—the three were an indivisible trinity.

Dostoevsky considered Russia uniquely qualified to lead a world reformation through Christ. Russia's mission consisted in giving Christ to the world, for Russia alone was the "god-bearing" nation. "Holy Russia" alone preserved the message undefiled, and therefore was eminently qualified to lead the universal renewal. Russia's "new word"—a phrase Dostoevsky was so fond of repeating—would change everything. Russia, after all, had been a servant to the world in many times past, sacrificing its needs and goals for others at its own expense. It would continue to be the servant of the world community. This world-changing process would begin with a Russian theocratic state imbued with Christian principles and policies. This state would indeed insure universal brotherhood. The star would rise in the East.

Dostoevsky lived in an age struggling with unusual stresses. His writings betray the dramatic tensions of that epoch. Old structures were crumbling, new and vital forces were attempting to assert themselves in an act of rampant nationalism and messianic claims. If Dostoevsky did no more then compensate Russian backwardness and inferiority by building up Russian self-esteem in his description of Russian spiritual development, he certainly over-fulfilled the task of negative critique of the West.

In his attack on the West, Dostoevsky often went beyond the

realm of historical reality. In this respect he was a victim of his own times. Masaryk points to a parallel in the Russian thought patterns of Dostoevsky's day; that is, Russian thought was all too often be negative, but not critically nuanced.[6]

Dostoevsky's virulent attack on the West, as we have seen in his *Winter Notes*, *The Idiot*, the *Diary* and *The Brothers Karamarov*, exemplifies his dichotomous approach. When he refers to the West, there is little of the ambiguity, duality, or oscillation that added strength and subtlety to his creative mastery elsewhere. For example, Turgenev became a mere personification of all that was despicable and ugly in Europe. Naturally, Dostoevsky's involuntary exiles, illnesses, and financial problems only exacerbated his conviction. At the time, we have seen, he feared losing touch with the real Russia and the subsequent loss of his own "cruel talent."

Although Dostoevsky occasionally made glowing remarks about Europe, this was not the essential Dostoevsky. Again, as Kohn observes, "theoretically Dostoevsky expressed sometimes an admiration for Europe, but it was always for a Europe gravely diseased or already dead."[7] In Dostoevsky's view Europe deserved to be destroyed because of its self-seeking, egotistical individualism, and its worn-out morals. Based on force, the misuse of power, pride, and violence, it was ready for burial. But as Saul Bellow says, "There is not a nation anywhere which does not contradict its highest principles in daily practice."[8]

Yet there certainly was much to condemn in Europe. When Dostoevsky expressed his convictions on the state of Orthodoxy, it is true, he often admitted that he was speaking of the Orthodox *ideal*. On occasion, however, his messianic impulses became excessive. He identified universal truth too closely with Russia, believing that Russia could assume the burden of the whole world. In thus isolating Russia from the rest of the Christian world, and associating the possibility of religious revival exclusively with Russia, Dostoevsky succumbed to Christian naturalism and utopianism.[9] I. S. Aksakov, an ardent Slavophile, portrayed the Orthodox Church of Dostoevsky's time more realistically.

> Generally speaking, among us in Russia, in Church affairs as in all other matters it is outward decorum that must be preserved at all costs; and with that our love for the Church, our idle love, our indo-

lent faith, is satisfied. We readily shut our eyes and, in our childish fear of scandal, attempt to blind ourselves and everyone else to all that great evil which under the veil of respectability is eating like a cancer into the living core of our religious organism.[10]

K. D. Kavelin (1818–85), an outstanding intellectual and westernizer of his time, in his dialog with Dostoevsky over the Western problem scored Dostoevsky's exaggerated claims for Russia.

Let me observe, in the first place, that one can hardly ascribe moral virtues to an entire people, especially when one belongs to it by birth, education, one's whole life, and all one's sympathies. What people does not consider itself the best, the most moral in the world! . . . You will extol the artlessness, meekness, humility, candor, kindness of the Russian people; someone else, with no less justification, will point out its bent for thieving, deceit, cheating, drink; the savage, revolting treatment of women. You will be given a multitude of examples of inhuman, ferocious cruelty.[11]

Dostoevsky's faith in the peasant, a class of society extolled for its meekness and humility, availed little to forestall the currents of the day. As Irvin Howe has remarked on the Slavophiles' view of the peasants, "their faith in the peasants is a sign of their distance from the peasants, their belief in a special Russian destiny a sign of their helplessness before the problems of Russia."[12] Still, Dostoevsky believed that the common people or masses, more than any other sector of Russian society, deserved to be called the people of God.

Dostoevsky's great love for his fellow Slavs was, on occasion, questionable. Referring time and time again to the great renewal of the world which Orthodoxy would lead from its own center, Dostoevsky's notion of brotherhood left something to be desired. As he wrote to Maikov in late winter of 1868, "But in order that this great object may be achieved, it is essential that the *political* right and supremacy of the Great-Russian rule over the whole Slav world should be definitively and uncontestably consummated." (*Pis'ma* 2:81.)

Dostoevsky's description of Orthodoxy and its means of achieving its self-imposed goals, were quite nebulous. Indeed, Dostoevsky has very little to say by way of positive, concrete paths toward developing its special vocation.[13] His goal, it appears, was to raise the national esteem of Russian Orthodoxy.

Dostoevsky's critique of the Catholic Church concentrates on several essential traits. If socialism represented secular compulsion, then the Pope and the Catholic Church represented theocratic compulsion. In the West only the shell or form of things past remained, but the content had substantially changed. The Roman Church, keeper of man's conscience, was therefore mentioned in the same breath with atheism, nihilism, and socialism. His attack on the Jesuits, moreover, as the conspirators *par excellence* in religious history was an indictment of spiritual misrepresentation. The West did not live under God, who was imprisoned by Rome, but under his false spokesmen, the Pope and his henchmen, the Jesuits.

In his enlightening study, Berdyayev refers to Dostoevsky as being "deeply chauvinistic," stating that "it must be admitted that Dostoevsky's knowledge of it [the Catholic Church] was neither deep nor exact."[14]

Kesich suggests that Dostoevsky's attack on the Catholic Church "is based on a limited conception. Dostoevsky derived his interpretation from statements of certain theologians who belonged to the Ultramontane party, and did not represent the mainstream of Catholic thinking even at the First Vatican Council of 1870."[15]

Certainly, Dostoevsky's knowledge was inadequate in the sense inasmuch as he was not a professional theologian or church historian, but his writing reflected far more than a simple bias dating from the deliberations of Vatican I. His interest, as this study shows clearly, precedes this period of history and represents an attitude current throughout the entire sweep of Russian tradition.

Dostoevsky's attack on the Church as being absorbed by the Pax Romana and the Church's authoritarian relationship to the world strikes a touchy point in the history of the Catholic Church. Unquestionably it became involved in, even enraptured by, the political scene. Far too often the Church was a political animal, vying for power with king and nation, a vulnerable spot of the Church of the West. The Church suffered a critical lack of a careful delineation and distinction of the Church's proper role in the world. "The Church has always existed within a state; and she has never arrived at a final and definitive statement of her relations with the state. The history of her relations with the state shows a bewildering variation of arrangements. The history of her theological understanding of her relations with the state shows scarcely less variation."[16]

On the possible merger of the Church with socialism, Dostoevsky was quite wrong. "Few fears now seem more absurd than his fear that Rome and socialism would band together against the Orthodox Church; yet he is unequalled in modern literature for showing the muddle that may lie beneath the order and precision of ideology."[17]

Concerning the Grand Inquisitor's interpretation of Christianity, especially the role of miracle, mystery and authority, Dostoevsky used Ivan's portrayal of extremism to score a point for the role of freedom. Dostoevsky quite naturally had no quarrel with these three essentials of any religious faith, but he certainly was aware of their extravagant abuses in history, notably in their usurpation at the expense of human freedom. This excess strikes at the inmost core of man, that is, at the enlightened freedom of man with respect. *"The Brothers Karamarov,* does *not* reject the view that man's three basic needs are (1) someone to worship, (2) someone to keep his conscience, and (3) some means of achieving universal unity. Moreover, Christianity does *not* reject miracle, mystery, and authority as means of satisfying those needs."[18]

In the place of the proper role of miracle, mystery, and authority, the Inquisitor offers magic, mystification, and tyranny. Contempt replaces equanimity and harmony with the human race.

> The Grand Inquisitor, who boldly undertook to correct Christ's work, is himself as weak and pitiful as the people whom he treats with such contempt. He made a dreadful miscalculation in appraising his role. He can tell but part of the truth—and not the most horrible part. The people accepted ideals from him indiscriminately, without examining them. That was only because, for the people, ideals are nothing more than a pastime, a decoration, a formality. Their childish, naive faith, which has not yet known doubt, demands nothing more for itself than a few words or other for its expression. That is why the people follow almost anyone who feels like leading them, and why they so readily change their idols: *le roi est mort, vive le roi.*[19]

Dostoevsky's critique of the Roman Church, to be sure, would have served far better purposes if he had not chosen to become so one-sided. Kavelin addressed this problem.

> In Catholicism, the creation of the Romance people's genius, you see

only the ugly organization of the Church after the pattern of a secular state, with a spiritual emperor at its heed, and in Protestantism, the conception of Christianity according to the spirit of the Germanic peoples, you see only the one-sided limitless freedom of individual thought, leading in the end to atheism; but Western Europe has produced much more than the pope and atheism under the unquestionable influence of Christianity. You contradict yourself when you admire European science, art, literature, in which the same spirit breathes that also produced both Catholic and Protestantism. To be consistent, you should reject all if you reject these—there is no middle ground.[20]

Kohn levels a similar criticism at Dostoevsky: he saw the danger which Western liberalism posed for the traditional ways of Russia, and thus tried to heighten faith in Russia, by comparing the imprefect and sordid realities of the West, to an ideal Russia existing in "lofty programs and daring anticipations." The Russian autocracy had few rivals in cruelty in war and oppression in peace.[21] Dostoevsky used a slavophile canard: he contrasted the historical expression of Catholicism and all its mistakes and shortcomings with an abstract and idealized version of Orthodoxy.[22]

Except for the sudden outburst in *The Idiot* and the *Legend of the Grand Inquisitor*, it is important to recall that Dostoevsky's harshest words of the West and the Catholic Church were in his *Diary*. As a publicist and journalist, he was at his passionate and polemical best. Issue-conscious, he displayed an absence of control and discipline that were evident in his more artistic creations. Often temperamental, he perhaps regretted some of the strong statements that came from his pen.

Yet, despite his own dark corners, Dostoevsky made his case for an untrammeled faith, unlittered with obstacles thrown in the way by human institutions. He stands uncorrected for

his belief that freedom of choice in the knowledge of good and evil is the essence of man's humanity and the essence of Christ's teaching. The kind of faith or obedience that is bought with bread is evil, and so is any constraint on man's conscience, in whatever form, even if this constraint is exercised for ostensibly good end. Freedom is not to be confounded with goodness or happiness. Goodness festers if bred by constraint, and happiness turns into brutish contentment. Only when freely chosen do they acquire a human content. This is precisely what makes Dostoevsky a novelist of tragic freedom, his perception that genuine freedom, being open to the choice of good and evil, is unthinkable without experiencing it, without substantiating it within the actual process of living.[23]

Although he grappled with Russia's traditional problems and groping for solutions for better days in a new society, Dostoevsky was not to be overcome by any false future endowed with complete happiness. He

> was not a believer in progress, and he condemned modern civilization as being materialistic and mechanistic. The end of history was not that of an earthly paradise, a vain and dangerous utopia, but the advent of the eternal city of God. In anticipation of that apocalyptic event, man's duty here on earth was to strive for the unity in Christ with his fellowman. All attempts to unify humanity on any other basis, by outward authority, by social and political reforms alone, or by appealing to utilitarian arguments, were bound to end in tragic failure.[24]

Dostoevsky firmly believed that the world could not do without a Rome, a conviction he expressed as far back as 1876 in the *Diary*, but the essential point he was making was that, whether in Geneva, Moscow, or Rome, the world needed a spiritual center based on Christ's love for all humanity, a love that was not debased with power politics and power struggles. This sensitive chord struck by Dostoevsky, a chord that has been muffled in the midst of so many other emotional and hyper-dramatic presentations, is the essential message of Dostoevsky. The appeal is as old as the New Testament itself. "Power should be the power of love and nothing else. Where the Church exhibits any other power as characteristic, both her members and others find it difficult to recognize her identity with the Church of the New Testament."[25]

NOTES

One
A Polemical Tradition

1. Samuel H. Cross and Olgerd Sherbowitz-Wetzor, trans. and eds., *The Russian Primary Chronicle: The Laurentian Text* (Cambridge: Mediaeval Academy of America, 1953). Interesting highlights on the early chronicle are found in Dmitrij Cizevskij, *History of Russian Literature* (The Hague: Mouton, 1960), 52–60, 101–9. *See also* George Vernadsky, *Kievan Russia*, vol. 2 of *A History of Russia* (New Haven: Yale University Press, 1948), 284–87.

2. Cross and Sherbowitz-Wetzor, *The Russian Primary Chronicle*, 53–54.

3. Francis Dvornik, *The Idea of Apostolicity in Byzantium and the Legend of the Apostle Andrew* (Cambridge: Harvard University Press, 1958), 3.

4. Nicholas Zernov, "Vladimir and the Origin of the Russian Church," *The Slavonic Review*, 38, No. 70 (November 1949), 126.

5. Henryk Paszkiewicz, *The Making of the Russian Nation* (London: Darton, Longman and Todd, 1963), 76, 90. *See also* Samuel H.

Cross, H. V. Morgilevski, and K. J. Conant, "The Earliest Mediaeval Churches of Kiev," *Speculum* 11 (1936): 477–99.

6. Francis Dvornik, "The Kiev State and its Relations with Western Europe," in *Transactions of the Royal Historical Society* (London: Butler and Tanner, 1947), 29:32.

7. Francis Dvornik, *The Making of Central and Eastern Europe* (London: The Polish Research Centre Ltd., 1959), 68.

8. Paszkiewicz, *The Making of the Russian Nation*, 90; Jozef Uminski, cited by Karolina Lanckoronska, *Studies on the Roman-Slavonic Rite in Poland* (Rome: Institutum Orientalium Studiorum, 1961), 157.

9. Martin Jugie, *Le schisme byzantin: aperçu historique et doctrinal* (Paris: P. Lethielleux, Libraire-Editeur, 1941), 174.

10. A. V. Kartashev, *Ocherki po istoriy russkoy tserkvi* (Paris: YMCA Press, 1959) 1:133–34.

11. *See* Metropolitan Makariy of Moscow [M. Bulgakov], *Istoriya russkoy tserkvi* (Saint Petersburg: Yuliya Andr. Bokrama, 1866–79), 1:220–52.

12. George Vernadsky, "The Status of the Russian Church During the First Half-Century Following Vladimir's Conversion," *Slavonic and East European Review* 20 (1941): 294. Paszkiewicz and Uminski hold the opinion already cited above in note 8.

13. *Chronicle*, 113.

14. A. A. Vasiliev, "Was Old Russia a Vassal State of Byzantium?" *Speculum* 7, No. 3 (July, 1932): 352. Noteworthy also is Ernest Honigmann, "Studies in Slavic Church History," *Byzantion* 17 (1944–45): 128–82. For a host of opinions and sources on the dependent nature of the early Kievan Church, *see The Russian Primary Chronicle*, 259–60. Also important in this connection is E. Golubinsky's two-volume, four-part study, *Istoriya russkoy tserkvi* (Moscow: Universitetskaia Tipografiya, Strastnoy Bul'var, 1901–11), especially 1,1:1–104.

15. *Primary Chronicle*, 111.

16. *Primary Chronicle*, 97.

17. *Primary Chronicle*, 113.

18. *Primary Chronicle*, no. 92, 245.

19. Zernov, "Vladimir and the Origin of the Russian Church," 429.

20. Henry Paszkiewicz, *The Origin of Russia* (London: Allen and Unwin, 1954), 107, 183.

21. Francis Dvornik, *The Slavs: Their Early History and Civilization* (Boston: American Academy of Arts and Sciences, 1956), 239 ff.

22. Kartashev, *Ocherki po istoriy Russkoy tservkvi* 1:263.

23. Dvornik, *The Slavs: Their Early History and Civilization*, 244.

24. William Medlin, *Moscow and East Rome: A Political Study of the Relations of Church and State in Muscovite Russia* (Geneva: Libraire E. Droz, 1952), 46, 53.

25. Paszkiewicz, *Origin of Russia*, 98.

26. N. K. Gudzy, *History of Early Russian Literature* (New York: Macmillan, 1949), 117.

27. Golubinsky, *Istoriya Russkoy tserkvi* 1,2:820–28.

28. Kartashev, *Ocherki po istoriy* 1:263–64.

29. Studies on this complex subject include Francis Dvornik, *Byzantine Political Ideas in Kievan Russia*, Dumbarton Oaks Papers, Nos. 9 and 10 (Cambridge: Harvard University Press, 1956), 73–121; Medlin, *Moscow and East Rome: A Political Study of the Relations of Church and State in Muscovite Russia*; Dimitri Obolensky, "Russia's Byzantine Heritage," *Oxford Slavonic Papers* 1 (1950): 37–63, and *Byzantium, Kiev and Moscow: A Study in Ecclesiastical Relations*, Dumbarton Oaks Papers, No. 11 (Cambridge: Harvard University Press, 1957), 21–78; Vasiliev, "Was Old Russia a Vassal State of Byzantium?"; George Vernadsky, "The Status of the Russian Church During the First Half-Century Following Vladimir's Conversion," *Slavonic and East European Review* 20 (1941): 294–314; Nicholas Zernov, "Vladimir and the Origin of the Russian Church," *The Slavonic Review* 28 (1949–50): 123–38; 425–38.

30. Yves Congar, O.P., *After Nine Hundred Years* (New York: Fordham University Press, 1959), 18.

31. Among the best commentaries on the rift between Rome and Byzantium are Congar, *After Nine Hundred Years*; Francis Dvornik, *Byzantium and the Roman Primacy* (New York: Fordham University Press, 1959); George Every, *The Byzantine Patriarchate: 451–1204* (London: SPCK, 1962); Jugie, *Le schisme byzantin*; Steven Runciman, *The Eastern Schism: A Study of the Papacy and the Eastern*

Churches during the XIth and XIIth Centuries (Oxford: Clarendon Press), 1955.

32. Golubinsky, *Istoriya russkoy tserkvi* 1,2:803.

33. Vernadsky, *Kievan Russia*, 270.

34. Steven Runciman, *A History of the Crusades* (Cambridge: Cambridge University Press, 1954), 3:123 ff.

35. Deno Geanakoplos, *Byzantine East and Latin West: Two Worlds of Christendom in Middle Ages and Renaissance* (New York: Barnes and Noble, 1966), 44.

36. Robert N. Bain, *Slavonic Europe* (Cambridge: Cambridge University Press, 1908), 12. *See also* Hermann Schreiber, *Teuton and Slav* (New York: Knopf, 1965) and Francis Dvornik, *The Slavs in European History and Civilization* (New Brunswick: Rutgers University Press, 1962), 20.

37. Vernadsky, *History of Russia* 3:55.

38. James H. Billington, *The Icon and the Axe* (New York: Knopf, 1966), 54.

39. G. P. Fedotov, *The Russian Religious Mind* (Cambridge: Harvard University Press, 1966) 2:1. *See also* Vernadsky, *History of Russia* 3:355–56.

40. Eric Voegelin, "The Mongol Orders of Submission to European Powers, 1245–1255," *Byzantion* 15 (1940–41): 409).

41. Vernadsky, *History of Russia* 3:131.

42. Fedotov, *The Russian Religious Mind* 2:11.

43. Vasiliev, "Was Old Russia a Vassal State of Byzantium?" 357.

44. Vernadsky, *History of Russia* 3:201.

45. Makariy, *Istoriya russkoy tserkvi* 5:326–27.

46. Vernadsky, *History of Russia* 5:32–33. *See also* the summary and highlights of the Jagellonian era in the fourteenth and early fifteenth centuries in Dvornik, *The Slavs: Their Early History and Civilization*, 212–31.

47. Kartashev, *Ocherki po istoriy russkoy tserkvi* 1:313 ff., describes the seeds of rivalry and disturbance within the Orthodox Church and consequent discord with the Catholic Church, all food for later and more bitter disputes.

48. Oswald Prentiss Backus, *Motives of West Russian Nobles in Deserting Lithuania for Moscow* (Lawrence: University of Kansas Press, 1957), 108.

49. Dvornik, *The Slavs in European History and Civilization*, 230–31.

50. Kartashev, *Ocherki po istoriy russkoy tserkvi* 1:321–48.

51. Oscar Halecki has the most concise treatment of the subject; particularly pertinent are his remarks in *From Florence to Brest: 1439–1596* (New York: Fordham University Press, 1958), 35–65. Also of importance for background is Joseph Gill, S.J., *The Council of Florence* (Cambridge: Cambridge University Press, 1959), 358–65. Gill in another study on Florence comments: "Isidore has always had what nowadays is called a bad press." *Personalities of the Council of Florence: And Other Essays* (New York: Barnes and Noble, 1964), 76.

52. Gill, *Council of Florence*, 265. *See also* Dvornik, *Byzantium and the Roman Primacy*, 13–14.

53. Deno J. Geanakopolos, "The Council of Florence (1438–1439) and the Problem of Union between the Greek and Latin Churches," *Church History* 24 (1955): 325.

54. Every, *The Byzantine Patriarchate (451–1204)*, 193. A standard work on this period is Paul Pierling, S.J., *La Russie et le Saint-Siège*, 5 vols. (Paris: Plon-Nourrit, 1901–12), especially 1:1–105.

55. Halecki, *From Florence to Brest: 1439–1596*, 62. Of special note is Michael Cherniavsky, "The Reception of the Council of Florence in Moscow," *Church History* 24 (1955): 347–59.

56. Gill, *The Council of Florence*, 361.

57. Ihor Sevcenko, "Intellectual Repercussions of the Council of Florence," *Church History* 24 (1955): 307.

58. Dvornik, *The Slavs in European History and Civilization*, 279.

59. Alexander V. Solovyov, *Holy Russia: The History of a Religious-Social Idea* (The Hague: Mouton and Co., 1959), 15.

60. Vasily N. Malinin, *Starets Eleazarova Monastyria Filofey i ego poslaniya* (Kiev: Tipografiya Kievo-Pecherskoy Uspenskoy Lavry, 1901), 99–100.

61. Dvornik, *The Slavs in European History and Civilization*, 388.

62. Steven Runciman, *The Fall of Constantinople 1453* (Cambridge: University Press, 1965), 178.

63. Paszkiewicz, *The Making of the Russian Nation*, 47.

64. Gudzy, *History of Early Russian Literature*, 257–58.

65. Gill, *The Council of Florence*, 396.

66. Kartashev, *Ocherki po istoriy russkoy tserkvi* 1:364–66; Dvornik, *The Slavs in European History and Civilization*, 262–65. Kartashev, *Ocherki po istoriy russkoy tserkvi* 1:531–675 and Makariy, *Istoriya russkoy tserkvi*, (vol. 9) are both devoted to the ecclesiastical era from the division of the metropolitanates until the Union of Brest in 1596.

67. Dvornik, *The Making of Central and Eastern Europe*, 260–61.

68. Steven Runciman, *The Great Church in Captivity: A Study of the Patriarchate of Constantinople from the Eve of the Turkish Conquest to the Greek War of Independence* (Cambridge: University Press, 1968), 321.

69. Medlin, *Moscow and East Rome*, 76.

70. Pierling, S.J., *La Russie et le Saint-Siège* 1: 171.

71. Medlin, *Moscow and East Rome*, 78.

72. Serge A. Zenkovsky, ed., *Medieval Russia's Epics, Chronicles, and Tales.* (New York: E. P. Dutton, 1963), 265–74; Gudzy, *History of Early Russian Literature*, 288–92.

73. Malinin, *Starets Eleazarova monastyria Filofey*, 45, 50–56. For further background and elaboration, *see* Dimitri Stremooukhoff, "Moscow the Third Rome: Sources of the Doctrine," *Speculum* 28 (1953): 84–101; Cyril Toumanoff, "Moscow the Third Rome; Genesis and Significance of a Politico-Religious Idea," *The Catholic Historical Review* 40 (1955): 411–47; Robert Lee Wolff, "The Three Romes: The Migration of an Ideology and the Making of an Autocrat," *Daedalus* 88 (1959): 291–311.

74. Cizevsky, *History of Russian Literature*, 300.

75. Medlin, *Moscow and East Rome*, 226.

76. Samuel S. Baron, ed. and trans., *The Travels of Olearius in Seventeenth-Century Russia* (Stanford: Stanford University Press, 1967), 283.

77. Philip I. Barbour, *Dimitry: Called the Pretender Tsar and Great Prince of All Russia, 1605–1606* (Boston: Houghton Mifflin, 1966) 142.

78. Cizevsky, *History of Russian Literature*, 300–306; Gudzy, *History of Early Russian Literature*, 341–48. The full title of the *Book of Degrees* reads in part: "Book of Degrees of the Imperial Genealogy of the Illustrious God-Ordained Scepter-holders Who Rule in Piety the Russian Land, and Who, Like the Groves of Paradise, Were Planted by God by the Water Springs and Given to Drink of Orthodoxy and Made to Grow in Wisdom and Grace, Who Were Irradiated by the Word of God Like a Luxuriant Orchard Which Is Fair with Leaves and Flowers, Abounding in Fruit Mellow and Full of Fragrance, Which Is Great and Tall, and Productive of Numerous Progeny, Spreads Magnificent and Is Extolled for Virtues Pleasing to God. . ." Gudzy, *History*, 345.

79. A. H. Hore, *History of the Greek Church* (London: James Parker and Co., 1902), 337–40, says that the patriarchate had to be purchased at the average rate of twenty-five thousand dollars. Robert N. Bain, *The First Romanovs (1613–1725)* (New York: Russell and Russell, 1967), 73.

80. Vernadsky, *A History of Russia* 4:273.

81. Kartashev, *Ocherki po istoriy russkoy tserkvi* 1:542, 589.

82. Cizevsky, *History of Russian Literature*, 231.

83. G. Fedotov, "Russia and Freedom," *Review of Politics* 8 (1946): 19.

84. Bjarne Nørretranders, *The Shaping of Czardom Under Ivan Groznyj* (Copenhagen: Munksgaard, 1964), 47.

85. J. L. I. Fennell, *The Correspondence between Prince A. M. Kurbsky and Tsar Ivan IV of Russia (1564–1579)* (Cambridge: Cambridge University Press, 1963), 15.

86. Bain, *The First Romanovs*, c. 3, "The Uniates and the Cossacks, 1580–1651," 68–95.

87. Vernadsky, *Russia at the Dawn of the Modern Age*, 279–89; *See also* Albert F. Pollard, *The Jesuits in Poland* (Oxford: B. H. Blackwell, 1892).

88. Zenkovsky, ed., *Medieval Russia's Epics, Chronicles, and Tales*, 277–88.

89. K. Waliszewski, *Ivan the Terrible* (Hamden, Conn.: Archon Books, 1966), 346. *See also* Pierling, S.J., *La Russie et le Saint-Siège* 2: 169.

90. Paul Miliukov, *Outlines of Russian Culture* (Philadelphia: University of Pennsylvania Press, 1948), 16.

91. Vernadsky, *Russia at the Dawn of the Modern Age*, 279. For glimpses of life in Muscovy as observed by foreigners during the second half of the sixteenth century, two works deserve special mention: Giles Fletcher, *Of the Rus Commonwealth*, edited by Albert E. Schmidt (Ithaca: Cornell University Press, 1966), especially 107–43, which focuses on the Russian Church, and Lloyd E. Berry, and Robert O. Crummey, eds., *Rude and Barbarous Kingdom: Russia in the Accounts of Sixteenth-Century English Voyagers* (Madison: University of Wisconsin Press, 1968).

92. Halecki, *From Florence to Brest: 1439–1596*, 381.

93. Kartashev, *Ocherki po istoriy russkoy tserkvi* 2:269.

94. Hore, *History of the Greek Church*, 413–14.

95. Dvornik, *The Slavs in European History and Civilization*, 473–74; Kartashev, *Ocherki po istoriy russkoy tserkvi* 1:624–75; Vernadsky, *Russia at the Dawn of the Modern Age*, 269–92. Halecki has the most pertinent background in *From Florence to Brest: 1439–1596*, 287–341 (preliminaries); 342–65 (opposition to the union); 366–91 (events of the synod itself). *See also* Pierling, *La Russie et le Saint-Siège*, vol. 2; Halecki, *From Florence to Brest: 1439–1596*, 211.

96. Kartashev, *Ocherki po istoriy russkoy tserkvi* 2:53.

97. Richard Pipes, ed., *Karamzin's Memoir on Ancient and Modern Russia* (Cambridge: Harvard University Press, 1959), 113–14.

98. Billington, *The Icon and the Axe*, 95–97 has incisive remarks on the collective psychology of this period.

99. Pipes, ed., *Karamzin's Memoir*, 114.

100. Zenkovsky, ed. *Medieval Russia's Epics, Chronicles, and Tales*, 302.

101. Zenkovsky, ed. *Medieval Russia's Epics*, 305–7.

102. Alexander Pushkin, *Boris Godunov*, trans. Alfred Hayes (New York: E. P. Dutton, 1918), 56.

103. Pushkin, *Boris Godunov*, 73.

104. Pushkin, *Boris Godunov*, 77.

105. Harold B. Segel, ed., *The Literature of Eighteenth Century Russia*, (New York: E. P. Dutton and Co., 1967), 399.

106. Segel, *The Literature of Eighteenth Century Russia*, 400.

107. Segel, *The Literature of Eighteenth Century Russia*, 434.

108. For background on the *Smutnoe vremya* or *Time of Troubles*, the following are worthy of mention: Billington, *The Icon and the Axe*, 101–10; Kartashev, *Ocherki po istoriy russkoy tserkvi* 2:53–54, emphasizes the role of the Jesuits in the campaign and that of the Poles: "The Jesuits were then governing the heart of Poland" (54); Medlin, *Moscow and East Rome*, 127 ff.; Dmitry Tolstoy, *Le catholicisme romain en Russie*, 2 vols. (Paris: Dentu, Libraire-Editeur, 1863, 1864), 1:71–108; Pierling, S.J., *La Russie et le Saint-Siège*, vol. 3; Vernadsky, *The Tsardom of Moscow 1547–1682*, vol. 5 of *A History of Russia*, part 1, 220–76; Warren B. Walsh, *Readings in Russian History* (Syracuse: Syracuse University Press, 1963), 1:109–31.

109. Medlin, *Moscow and East Rome*, 140.

110. Vernadsky, *The Tsardom of Moscow 1547–1682*, part 1, 454.

111. For a general overview of Russian Orthodoxy in Poland from Brest to unification with the Moscow Patriarchate in 1687, *see* Kartashev, *Ocherki po istoriy russkoy tserkvi* 2:267–97.

112. Runciman, *The Great Church in Captivity*, 348.

113. Bain, *The First Romanovs*, 90 ff.

114. Paul, Archdeacon of Aleppo, *The Travels of Macarius* (London: Oxford University Press, 1936), 15.

115. Paul, Archdeacon of Aleppo, *The Travels of Macarius*, 15.

116. Paul, Archdeacon of Aleppo, *The Travels of Macarius*, 17.

117. Paul, Archdeacon of Aleppo, *The Travels of Macarius*, 28.

118. Carl Bickford O'Brien, *Muscovy and the Ukraine: From the Pereiaslavl Agreement to the Truce of Andrusovo, 1654–1667* (Berkeley: University of California Press, 1963), 97–100.

119. Miliukov, *Outlines of Russian Culture*, 43. For this critical period in Russian history, *see also* Bain, *The First Romanovs*, 120–62; Michael Cherniavsky, *Tsar and People: Studies in Russian Myths* (New York: Random House, 1969), 61–71; Medlin, *Moscow and East Rome*, 139–210; and Archpriest Avvakum, *The Life of the Archpriest Avvakum by Himself* (Camden, Conn.: Archon Books, 1963). The most comprehensive work is William Palmer, *The Patriarch and the Tsar*, 6 vols. (London: Trubner and Co., 1871–76).

120. Solovyov, *Holy Russia: The History of a Religious-Social Idea*, 36.

121. Dmitry Tolstoy, *Le catholicisme romain en Russie* 1:111–15. Sophiya Buksgevden, *A Cavalier in Muscovy* (London: Macmillan, 1932), 315.

122. Sofiya Buksgevden, *Cavalier in Muscovy*, 315.

123. Jury Serech, "On Teofan Prokopovic as Writer and Preacher in His Kiev Period," *Harvard Slavic Studies*, vol. 7 (Cambridge: Harvard University Press, 1954), 215 ff.

124. Serech, "Teofan Prokopovic as Writer and Preacher in His Kiev Period," 216.

125. Kartashev, *Ocherki po istoriy russkoy tserkvi* 2:340.

126. L. R. Lewitter, "Peter the Great and the Polish Dissenters," *Slavonic and East European Review* 33:75–101; K. Waliszewski, *Peter the Great*, 2 vols. (New York: Haskell House, 1969), 1:120.

127. Hans Rogger, "The Russian National Character: Some Eighteenth-Century Views," *Harvard Slavic Studies*, vol. 4. (Cambridge: Harvard University Press, 1957), 22.

128. Thomas Campbell, S.J. *The Jesuits (1534–1921)*, 2 vols. (New York: The Encyclopedia Press, 1921), 2:641–64; Pierling, S.J., *La Russie et le Saint-Siège*, vol. 5, which extends coverage during the reigns of Catherine, Paul, and Alexander. Ludwig von Pastor, *The History of the Popes*, vols. 35–40 (London: Routledge and Kegan Paul, 1952), 39:162–76; 39:177–329.

129. Campbell, S.J. *The Jesuits: 1534–1921*, 2:641–64. Pierling, S.J., *La Russie et le Saint-Siège*, vol. 5; Pastor, *History of the Popes*, 39:177–329. *See also* Herbert H. Kaplan, *The First Partition of Poland* (New York: Columbia University Press, 1962), 191–95, on Catherine's declaration on behalf of the dissidents presented at the Diet of the Polish-Lithuanian Commonwealth on November 4, 1766.

130. Segel, *The Literature of Eighteenth Century Russia* 1:339.

131. Segel, *The Literature of Eighteenth Century Russia* 1:331.

132. Segel, *The Literature of Eighteenth Century Russia* 1:337.

133. Segel, *The Literature of Eighteenth Century Russia* 2:389.

134. Eduard Winter, *Russland und das Papsttum* (Berlin: Akademie-Verlag, 1961), 624–30.

135. K. Waliszewski, *Paul the First of Russia* (Hamden, Conn.: Archon Books, 1969), 178.

136. Michael Cherniavsky, *Tsar and People: Studies in Russian Myths* (New York: Random House, 1969), 132.

137. Paszkiewicz, *The Making of the Russian Nation*, 243, 224–25.

138. Waliszewski, *Ivan the Terrible*, 31.

139. Vernadsky, *The Mongols and Russia*, 153.

140. Michael Cherniavsky, *Tsar and People: Studies in Russian Myths* (New York: Random House, 1969), 1.

141. Marc Raeff, ed., *Russian Intellectual History: An Anthology* (New York: Harcourt, Brace and World, 1966), 56.

142. Hans Rogger, *National Consciousness in Eighteenth Century Russia* (Cambridge: Harvard University Press, 1960), 187–88. His most incisive remarks are found in chapter five, 186–252, "The Uses of History." According to most interpretations, eighteenth-century Russia was a much more secularized society than previous centuries.

143. Billington, *The Icon and the Axe*, 720.

144. Raeff, *Russian Intellectual History: An Anthology*, 8. See also Peter I. Chaadaev, *The Major Works of Peter Chaadaev*, trans. Raymond T. McNally (Notre-Dame: University of Notre Dame Press, 1969), 29–31, 200.

145. Michael B. Petrovich, *The Emergence of Russian Pan-Slavism (1856–1870)* (New York: Columbia University Press, 1958), 47.

146. Chaadayev, *The Major Works of Peter Chaadaev*, 29, 38.

147. V. F. Odoevsky, *Russian Nights* (New York: E. P. Dutton, 1965), 209–15.

148. Nikolay Lossky, *History of Russian Philosophy* (New York: International Universities Press, 1951), 38.

149. Nicholas V. Riasanovsky, *Russia and the West in the Teaching of the slavophiles: A Study of Romantic Ideology* (Cambridge: Harvard University Press, 1952), 90.

150. Peter K. Christoff, *An Introduction to Nineteenth-Century Russian Slavophilism* (The Hague: Mouton and Co., 1961), 94.

151. See W. J. Birkbeck, ed., *Russia and the English Church During the Last Fifty Years*, vol. 1: *Correspondence Between William Palmer*

and M. Khomiakoff (London: Rivington, Percival and Co., 1969). This contains a running correspondence between Khomyakov and William Palmer of Magdalen College in Oxford in the years 1844–54. Also pertinent is William Palmer, *Notes of a Visit to the Russian Church*, selected and arranged by Cardinal Newman (London: Longmans, Green and Co., 1895).

152. James E. Edie, James Scanlan, and Mary-Barbara Zeldin, eds. and trans., *Russian Philosophy*, 3 vols. (Chicago: Quadrangle, 1965), 1:174–75.

153. Raeff, *Russian Intellectual History: An Anthology*, 204–5, from Kireevski, "On the Nature of European Culture and Its Relation to the Culture of Russia," 175–207.

154. V. V. Zenkovsky, *A History of Russian Philosophy*, 2 vols. (London: Routledge and Kegan Paul, 1953), 1:236.

155. V. V. Zenkovsky, *Russian Thinkers and Europe* (Ann Arbor: J. W. Edwards, 1953), 49.

156. Zenkovsky, *Russian Thinkers and Europe*, 84.

157. Riasanovsky, *Russia and the West in the Teaching of the Slavophiles*, 97.

158. Zenkovsky, *Russian Thinkers and Europe*, 53.

159. Nicolas Zernov, *Three Russian Prophets: Khomiakov, Dostoevsky, Soloviev* (London: SCM Press, 1944), 53.

160. Alexander Herzen, *My Past and Thoughts*, vols. 2, 3 (London: Chatto and Windus, 1924), 3:38. After becoming disillusioned with the European revolution of 1848, Herzen declared that the West was dying.

161. Robert E. MacMaster, *Danilevsky: A Russian Totalitarian Philosopher* (Cambridge: Harvard University Press, 1967), 231.

Two

Dostoevsky: *Prophet of Russian Orthodoxy*

1. Nadejda Gorodetzky, *The Humiliated Christ in Modern Russian Thought* (New York: Macmillan, 1938), x.

2. Vladimir S. Solovyov, *Sobranie sochineny* (Saint Petersburg: Izdanie Tovarishchestva 'Obshchestvennaia Pol'za7, 1901), 3:174, 182.

3. Konstantin Mochulsky, *Dostoevsky: His Life and Work* (Princeton: Princeton University Press, 1967), xix.

4. Dmitri S. Merezhkovsky, *Tolstoy as Man and Artist: With an Essay on Dostoevsky* (New York: G. P. Putnam's Sons, 1902), 3.

5. Nicholas Berdyayev, *Dostoevsky* (New York: Meridian, 1957), 35.

6. Aimée Dostoevsky, *Fyodor Dostoevsky: A Study* (New Haven: Yale University Press, 1922), 1–7; Mochulsky, *Dostoevsky*, 3; Avrahm Yarmolinsky, *Dostoevsky: Works and Days* (New York: Funk and Wagnalls, 1971), 6; Stanislaw Mackiewicz, *Dostoevsky* (New York: Haskell House, 1974), 61; Joseph Frank, *Dostoevsky: The Seeds of Revolt, 1821–1849* (Princeton: Princeton University Press, 1976), 8.

7. Fyodor Dostoevsky, *The Diary of a Writer*, tran. Boris Brasol. 2 vols. (New York: Charles Scribner's Sons, 1949), 1:152.

8. Avrahm Yarmolinsky, *Dostoevsky: His Life and Art* (New York: Criterion Books, 1957), 1; Mochulsky, *Dostoevsky*, 8.

9. Fyodor Dostoevsky, *Biografiya pis'ma i zametki iz zapisnoy knizhi F. M. Dostoyevskogo* (St. Petersburg: Tipografiya A. S. Suvorina, 1883), 18–19; Jessie Coulson, *Dostoevsky: A Self-Portrait* (New York: Oxford University Press, 1962), 6.

10. Mochulsky, *Dostoevsky*, 8.

11. Jessie Coulson, *Dostoevsky: A Self-Portrait* (New York: Oxford University Press, 1962), 29.

12. Coulson, *Dostoevsky*, 29.

13. René Wellek, ed. *Dostoevsky: A Collection of Critical Essays* (Englewood Cliffs, N. J.: Prentice-Hall, Inc., 1962), 1.

14. E. J. Simmons, *Dostoevsky: The Making of a Novelist* (New York: Oxford University Press, 1940), 63.

15. Nicholas V. Riasanovsky, "Fourierism in Russia: An Estimate of the Petrassevcy." *American Slavic and East European Review* 12 (1953): 289–302.

16. Simmons, *Dostoevsky* 64.

17. Avrahm Yarmolinsky, *Dostoevsky: A Study in His Ideology* (New York, n. p., 1921), especially 14–19.

18. Simmons, *Dostoevsky*, 61.

19. Simmons, *Dostoevsky*, 65.

20. Hans Kohn, *Prophets and Peoples: Studies in Nineteenth Century Nationalism* (New York: Macmillan, 1946), 148.

21. A. P. Milyukov is cited in *Letters of Fyodor Dostoevsky to His Family and Friends*, trans. E. C. Mayne (New York: Horizon Press, 1961), 273.

22. Mochulsky, *Dostoevsky*, 125–26.

23. Vissarion G. Belinsky, *Selected Philosophical Works* (Moscow: Foreign Languages Publishing House, 1956), 537–40.

24. Nikolay Gogol, *Letters*, edited by Carl R. Proffer (Ann Arbor: The University of Michiagan Press, 1967), 177.

25. Yarmolinsky, *Dostoevsky: His Life and Art*, 15.

26. This is taken from the memoranda of P. K. Martyanov.

27. W. H. Carr, "Was Dostoevsky an Epileptic?" *The Slavonic Review* 9 (1930): 424–31.

28. The identification of the convict as Aley is from Mochulsky, *Dostoevsky*, 192.

29. Mochulsky, *Dostoevsky*, 153.

30. Mochulsky, *Dostoevsky*, 157.

31. Michael Cherniavsky has some stimulating thoughts on this in *Tsar and People*, 202–5.

32. Simmons, *Dostoevsky*, 74.

33. Zenkovsky, *A History of Russian Philosophy* 1:414. *Vremya* thus competed with *Fatherland Notes*, (Dostoevsky's own contributing source), *The Contemporary* (Chernyshevsky replacing Belinsky), *The Russian Herald*, *The Russian World* (for radical views), and *The Bell* (Herzen as editor).

34. Lev Shestov, *Athens and Jerusalem* (Athens: Ohio University Press, 1966), 329.

35. Michael Karpovich, "Tolstoy and Dostoevsky—Two Spokesmen for Russia," *World Literatures*, ed. Joseph Remenyi (Freeport, N. Y.: Books for Libraries Press, 1968), 250.

36. Coulson, *Dostoevsky*, 111.

37. Riasanovsky, *Russia and the West in the Teaching of the Slavophiles*, 75, 120.

38. Zenkovsky, *A History of Russian Philosophy* 1:179.

39. Gogol, *Letters of Nikolai Gogol*, 193.

40. Zenkovsky, *A History of Russian Philosophy* 1:191.

41. *See* N. V. Riasanovsky, "Khomiakov on Sobornost," in Christoff, ed., *Introduction to Nineteenth-Century Russian Slavophilism*; Edie, Scanlan, and Zeldin, *Russian Philosophy* 1:157–64; E. J. Simmons, ed., *Continuity and Change in Russian and Soviet Thought* (Cambridge: Harvard University Press, 1955), 183–96; Nikolay Lossky, *History of Russian Philosophy* (New York: International Universities Press, 1951), 15–41; Nicolas Zernov, *Three Russian Prophets*, 48–81; Zenkovsky, *History of Russian Philosophy*, 1.

42. Cherniavsky, *Tsar and People*, 202. Also interesting, from another aspect, is Maria Kravchenko, *Dostoevsky and the Psychologists* (Amsterdam: Hakkert, 1978), 165.

43. Kohn, *Prophets and Peoples*, 140.

44. *See above*, 000.

45. Dostoevsky expressed this theme five years earlier: the masses maintain "the firm belief that Russia exists for the sole purpose of serving Christ and protecting ecumenic orthodoxy as a whole." *Diary* [December 1876], 1:555.

46. Mochulsky, *Dostoevsky*, 573.

47. Mochulsky, *Dostoevsky*, 635. *See* Nadejda Gorodetzky, *Saint Tikhon Zadonsky: Inspirer of Dostoevsky* (London: SPCK, 1951), vii. There is a variety of opinion on the sources of Dostoevsky's portrayal of Zossima, but today there is wide agreement that the figure is heavily drawn from the real Father Ambrose. Gorodetzky takes a counter position (180–88). Dostoevsky's daughter referred to the personality of Ambrose as the basis for Zossima. Aimée Dostoevsky, *Fyodor Dostoevsky*, 232. *See also* Dmitry F. Grigorieff, "Dostoevsky's Elder Zossima and the Real Life Father Amvrosy." *St. Vladimir's Seminary Quarterly* 11 (1967): 22–34.

48. Riasanovsky, *Russia and the West in the Teaching of the Slavophiles*, 206.

49. Solovyov, *Sobranie sochineny* 3:180–81.

50. Solovyov, *Sobranie sochineny* 3:200.

51. *See* the pertinent, though slightly exaggerated, analysis of this passage in David Magarshack, *Dostoevsky* (London: Secker & Warburg, 1962), 462.

Three
Dostoevsky and the Catholic Pax Romana

1. Simmons, *Dostoevsky*, 124.

2. The citation is to Fonvizin's letter to P. Panin, September 29, 1778.

3. *See above*, 000.

4. Marc Slonin, *Three Loves of Dostoevsky* (London: Alvin Redman, 1957), 131.

5. Anna Dostoevsky, *Dostoevsky Portrayed by His Wife: The Diary and Reminiscences of Mme. Dostoevsky*, S. S. Koteliansky, tran. (New York: E. P. Dutton and Co., 1926), 136.

6. Avram Yarmolinsky, *Turgenev the Man, His Art and His Age* (New York: The Orion Press, 1959), 275.

7. *Dostoevsky Portrayed by His Wife*, 211.

8. *Dostoevsky Portrayed by His Wife*, 210.

9. *Dostoevsky Portrayed by His Wife*, 211.

10. *Dostoevsky Portrayed by his Wife*, 135.

11. Hugh Seton-Watson, *The Russian Empire 1801–1917* (Oxford: Clarendon Press), 742.

12. Zenkovsky, *Russian Thinker and Europe*, 168.

13. Aimée Dostoevsky, *Fyodor Dostoevsky*, 255.

14. *See also* below, 000.

15. Anna Dostoevsky relates that her husband went to the Kazan cathedral on hearing of the Russian entry into Turkey and spent a half hour in prayer for Russia's cause. Mochulsky, *Dostoevsky*, 541.

16. *See* Dostoevsky's letters to Maykov of December 12/23, 1868, and March 25/April 6, 1870.

17. Curle, *Characters of Dostroevsky*, 180.

18. Curle, *Characters of Dostoevsky*, 176.

19. Sigmund Freud, "Dostoevsky and Parricide," in *Dostoevsky: A Collection of Critical Essays*, René Wellek, ed. (Englewood Cliffs, N. J.: Prentice-Hall, Inc., 1962), 98.

20. Romano Guardini, "The Legend of the Grand Inquisitor," *Cross Currents* 3 (1956): 58–86.

21. Veselin Kesich, "Some Religious Aspects of Dostoevsky's 'Brothers Karamazov,'" *St. Vladimir's Seminary Quarterly* 9 (1965): 93.

22. Curle, *Characters of Dostoevsky*, 177.

23. Philip Rahv, *The Myth and the Powerhouse* (New York: Farrar, Straus and Giroux, 1965), 145.

24. Nicholas Berdyayev, *The Russian Idea* (New York: Macmillan, 1948), 122, 153.

25. Kesich, "Some Religious Aspects of Dostoevsky's *Brothers Karamazov*," 84–86.

26. Ellis Sandoz, *The Grand Inquisitor: A Study in Political Apocalypse*, (N.P., 1967), 233.

27. Romano Guardini, "Legend of the Grand Inquisitor," 60, 85.

28. Guardini, "Legend of the Grand Inquisitor," 62.

29. Mochulsky, *Dostoevsky*, 622.

30. Zenkovsky, *Russian Thinkers and Europe*, 167.

31. D. H. Lawrence, "Preface to Dostoevsky's The Grand Inquisitor," in *Dostoevsky: A Collection of Critical Essays*, 90.

32. Curle, *Characters of Dostoevsky*, 199.

33. Guardini, "The Legend of the Grand Inquisitor," 62.

34. Rahv, *The Myth and the Powerhouse*, 145.

35. René Fülöp-Miller, *The Power and Secret of the Jesuits* (New York: Viking Press, 1930), 466.

36. Fülöp-Miller, *Power and Secret of the Jesuits*, 466–67.

37. Fülöp-Miller, *Power and Secret of the Jesuits*, 467.

38. Rahv, *The Myth and the Powerhouse*, 155.

39. Edward Wasiolek, ed., *"The Brothers Karamazov" and the Critics* (Belmont, Calif.: Wadsworth Publishing Co., 1967), 130.

40. Nikolay Lossky, *Dostoevsky i ego hristianskoe miroponimanie* (New York: Izdatel'stvo Imeni Chehova, 1953), 361. Guardini holds a similar view; *see* "Legend of the Grand Inquisitor," 61.

Conclusion

1. Hugh Seton-Watson, *The Russian Empire 1801–1917*, 740.

2. Clarence A. Manning, "Dostoevsky and Scythism," *Sewanee Review* 33 (April 1925), 135.

3. Kohn, *Prophets and Peoples*, 135.

4. Karpovich, "Tolstoy and Dostoevsky—Two Spokesmen for Russia," 241–42.

5. Philip Mosely, in *Continuity and Change in Russian and Soviet Thought*, E. J. Simmons, ed., (Cambridge: Harvard University Press, 1955), 553.

6. Masaryk is cited in Hans Kohn, *Pan-Slavism: Its History and Ideology* (Notre-Dame: University of Notre Dame Press, 1953), 286.

7. Kohn, *Prophets and Peoples*, 199.

8. Saul Bellow, "Foreword" to Fyodor Dostoevsky, *Winter Notes on Summer Impressions*, Richard Lee Renfield, tran. (New York: Criterion Books, 1955), 20.

9. Zenkovsky, *Russian Thinkers and Europe*, 170.

10. I. S. Aksakov, "On the Official Church in Russia," in *Russia and the Universal Church*, V. S. Solovyov, ed. (London: Goeffrey Bles, 1948), 66.

11. Konstantin D. Kavelin, "A Letter to Dostoevsky," *Russian Intellectual History: An Anthology*, Marc Raeff, ed. (New York: Harcourt, Brace and World, 1966), 310–11.

12. Irving Howe, *Politics and the Novel* (New York: Horizon Press, 1957), 53.

13. Zenkovsky, *A History of Russian Philosophy* 1:431.

14. Nicholas Berdyayev, *Dostoevsky*, 146. Berdyayev cautions his readers again about Dostoevsky's inadequate knowledge on page 200.

15. Vesilin Kesich, "Some Religious Aspects of Dostoevsky's 'Brothers Karamazov.'" *St. Vladimir's Seminary Quarterly* 9 (1965): 85.

16. John L. McKenzie, S.J., *The Power and the Wisdom: An Interpretation of the New Testament* (Milwaukee: Bruce, 1965), 282.

17. Howe, *Politics and the Novel*, 71.

18. Roger L. Cox, *Between Earth and Heaven: Shakespeare, Dostoevsky, and the Meaning of Christian Tragedy* (New York: Holt, Rinehart and Winston, 1969), 195.

19. Lev Shestov, "Dostoevsky and Nietzsche; The Philosophy of Tragedy," in *Essays in Russian Literature—The Conservative View:*

Leontiev, Rozanov, Shestov, Spencer E. Roberts, ed. (Athens: Ohio University Press, 1968), 77.

20. Kavelin, "A Letter to Dostoevsky," 314.

21. Kohn, *Pan-Slavism: History and Ideology,* 168.

22. Riasanovsky, *Russia and the West in the Teaching of the Slavophiles,* 197.

23. Rahv, *The Myth and the Powerhouse,* 172.

24. Karpovich, "Tolstoy and Dostoevsky—Two Spokesmen for Russia," 250.

25. McKenzie, *The Power and the Wisdom,* 282.

BIBLIOGRAPHY

Primary Sources

Dostoevsky, Fyodor. *The Best Short Stories of Dostoevsky*. Translated by David Magarshack. New York: Modern Library, 1964.

——. *Biografiya, pis'ma i zametki iz zapisnoy knizhi F. M. Dostoyevskogo.* [Biography, letters, and notes from the notebooks of F. M. Dostoevsky.] St. Petersburg: Tipografiya A. S. Suvorina, 1883.

——. *The Brothers Karamazov.* Translated by Constance Garnett. New York: Modern Library, 1950.

——. *Crime and Punishment.* New York: Bantam, 1962.

——. *The Diary of a Writer.* Translated by Boris Brasol. 2 vols. New York: Charles Scribner's Sons, 1949.

——. *Dostoevsky's Occasional Writings.* Translated by David Magarshack. New York: Random House, 1963.

——. *The Dream of a Queer Fellow* and *The Pushkin Speech.* Translated by S. Koteliansky and J. Middleton Murry. New York: Barnes and Noble, 1961.

———. *The Gambler. Bobok. A Nasty Story.* Translated by Jessie Coulson. Baltimore: Penguin Books, 1966.

———. *The House of the Dead.* New York: Dell, 1965.

———. *The Idiot.* Translated by Constance Garnett. New York: Macmillan, 1948.

———. *The Insulted and Injured.* New York: Grove Press, 1955.

———. *Letters and Reminiscences.* Translated by S. Koteliansky and J. M. Murry. New York: Alfred A. Knopf, 1923.

———. *The Letters of Dostoevsky to His Wife.* With Introduction by D. S. Mirsky. London: Constable and Co., 1930.

———. *Letters of Fyodor Dostoevsky To His Family and Friends.* Translated by E. C. Mayne, with Introduction by Avrahm Yarmolinsky. New York: Horizon Press, 1961.

———. *Materialy i issledovaniya.* [Documents and research.] Edited by A. S. Iskoz [A. S. Dolinin]. Leningrad: Izdatel'stvo Akademiy Nauk SSSR, 1935.

———. *Memoirs from the House of the Dead.* Translated by Jessie Coulson. New York: Oxford University Press, 1965.

———. *New Dostoyevsky Letters.* Translated by S. Koteliensky. London: Mandrake Press, 1927.

———. *The Notebooks for "Crime and Punishment."* Edited and translated by Edward Wasiolek. Chicago: University of Chicago Press, 1967.

———. *The Notebooks for "The Brothers Karamazov."* Edited by Edward Wasiolek. Chicago: University of Chicago Press, 1971.

———. *The Notebooks for "The Idiot."* Edited by Edward Wasiolek and translated by Katherine Strelsky. Chicago: University of Chicago Press, 1967.

———. *The Notebooks for "The Possessed."* Edited by Edward Wasiolek and translated by Victor Terras. Chicago: University of Chicago Press, 1968.

———. *The Notebooks for "A Raw Youth."* Edited by Edward Wasiolek and translated by Victor Terras. Chicago: University of Chicago Press, 1969.

———. *Notes from Underground* and *The Grand Inquisitor.* Translated by Ralph E. Matlaw. New York: E. P. Dutton and Co., 1960

_____ . *Notes from Underground, Poor People*, and *The Friend of the Family*. New York: Dell, 1967.

_____ . *Pages from the Journal of an Author*. Translated by S. Koteliansky and J. M. Murry. London: Maunsel and Co., 1916.

_____ . *Pis'ma*. [Letters.] 4 vols. Moscow: Gosudarstvennoe Izdatel'stvo, 1938, 1930, 1934, 1959.

_____ . *The Possessed*. Translated by Andrew R. MacAndrew. New York: New American Library, 1962.

_____ . *A Raw Youth*. Translated by Constance Garnett. New York: Macmillan, 1950.

_____ . *Stat'i i materialy*. [Articles and essays.] Edited by A. S. Iskoz [A. S. Dolinin]. St. Petersburg: Tseatral'noe Kooperativnoe Izdatel'stvo, 'Mysl,' 1922.

_____ . *Summer Impressions*. Translated by Kyril Fitzlyon. London: John Calder, 1955.

_____ . *Vremya*. [Time.] Vol. 1 (1861); Vol. 2 (1862).

_____ . *Winter Notes on Summer Impressions*. Translated by Richard Lee Renfield. New York: Criterion Books, 1955.

Secondary Sources

Avvakum, Archpriest. *The Life of the Archpriest Avvakum by Himself*. Camden, Conn.: Archon Books, 1963.

Backus, Oswald Prentiss. *Motives of West Russian Nobles in Deserting Lithuania for Moscow*. Lawrence: University of Kansas Press, 1957.

Bain, Robert N. *The First Romanovs (1613–1725)*. New York: Russell and Russell, 1967.

_____ . *Slavonic Europe: A Political History of Poland and Russia from 1447 to 1796*. Cambridge: Cambridge University Press, 1908.

Barbour, Philip I. *Dimitry: Called the Pretender Tsar and Great Prince of All Russia, 1605–1606*. Boston: Houghton Mifflin, 1966.

Baron, Pierre. *Un theologien léic orthodoxe Russe au xixieme siecle: Alexis Stepanovitch Khomiakov (1804–1860)*. [A nineteenth-century Russian Orthodox lay theologian: Alexis Stepanovich Khomyakov (1804–1860).] Orientalia Christiana Analecta, no.

127. Rome: Pontificum Institutum Orientalium Studiorum, 1940.

Baynes, H. H., and H. Moss, eds. *Byzantium: An Introduction to East Roman Civilization.* Oxford: Clarendon Press, 1949.

Belinsky, Vissarion G. *Selected Philosophical Works.* Moscow: Foreign Languages Publishing House, 1956.

Berdyayev, Nikolay. *Dostoevsky.* New York: Meridian Books, 1957.

——. *The Origin of Russian Communism.* London: Geoffrey Bles, 1948.

——. *The Russian Idea.* New York: Macmillan, 1948.

Berry, Lloyd E. and Robert O. Crummey, eds. *Rude and Barbarous Kingdom: Russia in the Accounts of Sixteenth-Century English Voyagers.* Madison: University of Wisconsin Press, 1968.

Billington, James H. *The Icon and the Axe: An Interpretive History of Russian Culture.* New York: Alfred Knopf, 1966.

——. "Images of Muscovy." *Slavic Review* 21 (1962): 24–34.

Birkbeck, W. J., ed. *Russia and the English Church During the Last Fifty Years.* Vol. 1: *Correspondence Between William Palmer and M. Khomiakoff.* London: Rivington, Percival and Co., 1969.

Buksgevden, Sophia. *A Cavalier in Muscovy.* London: Macmillan, 1932.

Campbell, Thomas, S.J. *The Jesuits (1534–1921).* 2 vols. New York: The Encyclopedia Press, 1921.

Carr, Edward Hallett. "Was Dostoyevsky an Epileptic?" *The Slavonic Review* 9 (1930): 424–31.

Chaadaev, Peter Y. *The Major Works of Peter Chaadaev.* Translated by Raymond T. McNally. Notre-Dame: University of Notre Dame Press, 1969.

Cherniavsky, Michael. "The Reception of the Council of Florence in Moscow." *Church History* 24 (1955): 347–59.

——. *Tsar and People: Studies in Russian Myths.* New York: Random House, 1969

Christoff, Peter K. *An Introduction to Nineteenth-Century Russian Slavophilism.* Vol. 1: A. S. Khomiakov. The Hague: Mouton and Co., 1961.

Cizevskij, Dmitrij. *History of Russian Literature: From the Eleventh Century to the End of the Baroque.* The Hague: Mouton and Co., 1960.

Congar, Yves, O.P. After Nine Hundred Years. New York: Fordham University Press, 1959.

Coulson, Jessie. *Dostoevsky: A Self-Portrait.* New York: Oxford University Press, 1962.

Cox, Roger L. *Between Earth and Heaven: Shakespeare, Dostoevsky, and the Meaning of Christian Tragedy.* New York: Holt, Rinehart and Winston, 1969.

Cross, Samuel. "Mediaeval Russian Contacts with the West." *Speculum* 10 (1935): 137–44.

Cross, Samuel, B. V. Morgilevski, and K. J. Conant. "The Earliest Mediaeval Churches of Kiev." *Speculum* 11 (1936): 477–99.

Cross, Samuel, and Olgerd Sherbowitz-Wetzor, trans. and eds. *The Russian Primary Chronicle: The Laurentian Text.* Cambridge: Mediaeval Academy of America, 1953.

Crowther, Peter A., ed. *A Bibliography of Works in English on Early Russian History to 1800.* New York: Barnes and Noble, 1969.

Curle, Richard. *Characters of Dostoevsky: Studies from Four Novels.* New York: Russell and Russell, 1966.

Dostoevsky, Anna. *Bibliograficheskiy ukazatel' (F. M. Dostoyevskago).* [Biographical index of F. M. Dostoevsky.] Saint Petersburg: Tipografiya P. T. Panteleeva, 1906.

———. *Dostoevsky Portrayed by His Wife: The Diary and Reminiscences of Mme. Dostoevsky.* Translated by S. S. Koteliansky. New York: E. P. Dutton and Co., 1926.

———. *The Diary of Dostoevsky's Wife.* Edited by René Fülöp-Miller and F. Eckstein. New York: Macmillan, 1928.

Dostoyevsky, Lubov [Aimée]. *Fedor Dostoyevsky: A Study.* New Haven: Yale University Press, 1922.

Dvornik, Francis. *Byzantine Missions Among the Slavs: SS. Constantine-Cyril and Methodius.* New Brunswick: Rutgers University Press, 1970.

———. "Byzantine Political Ideas in Kievan Russia." *Dumbarton Oaks Papers.* Nos. 9, 10. Cambridge: Harvard University Press, 1956.

———. *Byzantium and the Roman Primacy.* New York: Fordham University Press, 1966.

———. *Early Christian and Byzantine Political Philosophy: Origins and Background.* 2 vols. Washington, D.C.: Dumbarton Oaks Center for Byzantine Studies, 1966.

———. *The Idea of Apostolicity in Byzantium and the Legend of the Apostle Andrew.* Cambridge: Harvard University Press, 1958.

———. "The Kiev State and its Relations with Western Europe" *Transactions of the Royal Historical Society.* Vol. 29. London: Butler and Tanner, Ltd., 1947.

———. *The Making of Central and Eastern Europe.* London: The Polish Research Centre, 1949.

———. *The Slavs in European History and Civilization.* New Brunswick: Rutgers University Press, 1962.

———. *The Slavs: Their Early History and Civilization.* Boston: American Academy of Arts and Sciences, 1956.

Edie, James M., James Scanlan, and Mary-Barbara Zeldin, eds. *Russian Philosophy.* 3 vols. Chicago: Quadrangle, 1965.

Every, George, S.S.M. *The Byzantine Patriarchate: 451–1204.* London: SPCK, 1962.

Fedotov, George. P. "Russia and Freedom." *Review of Politics* 8 (1950): 12–36.

———. *The Russian Religious Mind.* Vol. 1: *Kievan Christianity: The Tenth to Thirteenth Centuries.* New York: Harper and Row, 1960.

———. *The Russian Religious Mind.* Vol. 2: *The Middle Ages: The Thirteenth to the Fifteenth Centuries.* Cambridge: Harvard University Press, 1966.

———. *A Treasury of Russian Spirituality.* New York: Sheed and Ward, 1950.

Fennell, John L. I. *The Correspondence between Prince A. M. Kurbsky and Tsar Ivan IV of Russia (1564–1579).* Cambridge: University Press, 1963.

Fletcher, Giles. *Of the Rus Commonwealth.* Edited by Albert E. Schmidt. Ithaca: Cornell University Press, 1966.

Frank, Joseph. *Dostoevsky: The Seeds of Revolt, 1821–1849.* Princeton: Princeton University Press, 1976.

Fülöp-Miller, René. *Fyodor Dostoevsky: Insight, Faith, and Prophecy.* New York: Charles Scribner's Sons, 1950.

———. *The Power and Secret of the Jesuits.* New York: Viking Press, 1930.

Geanakoplos, Deno J. *Byzantine East and Latin West: Two Worlds of Christendom in Middle Ages and Renaissance.* New York: Barnes and Noble, 1966.

____ . "The Council of Florence (1438–1439) and the Problem of Union between the Greek and Latin Churches." *Church History* 24 (1955): 324–46.

Gill, Joseph, S.J. *The Council of Florence.* Cambridge: Cambridge University Press, 1959.

____ . *Eugenius IV, Pope of Christian Union.* Westminster, Md.: The Newman Press, 1961.

____ . *Personalities of the Council of Florence And Other Essays.* New York: Barnes and Noble, 1964

Gogol, Nikolay V. *Letters of Nikolai Gogol.* Edited by Carl R. Proffer. Ann Arbor: University of Michigan Press, 1967.

____ . *Polnoe sobranie sochineniy.* [Complete works.] Vol. 8. Moscow: I. N. Kushnerev, 1912.

Golubinsky, E. *Istoriya russkoy tserkvi.* [History of the Russian church.] 2 vol., each in two parts. Moscow: Universitetskaia Tipografiya, Strastnoy Bul'var, 1901–11.

Gordon, Patrick. *Passages from the Diary of General Patrick Gordon of Auchleuchries: In the Years 1635–1699.* London: Frank Cass and Co., 1968. "Russia through European Eyes Series."

Gorodetzky, Nadejda. *The Humiliated Christ in Modern Russian Thought.* New York: Macmillan, 1938.

____ . *Saint Tikhon Zadonsky: Inspirer of Dostoevsky.* London: SPCK, 1951.

Graham, Hugh F. "Peter Mogila—Metropolitan of Kiev." *Russian Review* 14 (1955): 345–56.

Grigorieff, Dmitry F. "Dostoevsky's Elder Zosima and the Real Life Father Amvrosy." *St. Vladimir's Seminary Quarterly* 11 (1967): 22–34.

Guardini, Romano. "The Legend of the Grand Inquisitor." *Cross Currents* 3 (1956): 58–86.

Gudzy, Nikolay K. *History of Early Russian Literature.* New York: Macmillan, 1949.

Halecki, Oscar. *From Florence to Brest: 1439–1596.* New York: Fordham University Press, 1958.

Herzen, Alexander. *My Past and Thoughts.* Vols. 2, 3. London: Chatto and Windus, 1924.

Honigmann, Ernest. "Studies in Slavic Church History." *Byzantion* 17 (1944–45): 128–82.

Hore, A. H. *History of the Greek Church.* London: James Parker and Co., 1902.

Howe, Irving. *Politics and the Novel.* New York: Horizon Press, 1957.

Jugie, Martin. *Le schisme byzantin: aperçu historique et doctrinal.* [The Byzantine schisme: a historical and doctrinal survey]. Paris: P. Lethielleux, Libraire-Editeur, 1941.

Kaplan, Herbert H. *The First Partition of Poland.* New York: Columbia University Press, 1962.

Karpovich, Michael. "Tolstoy and Dostoevsky—Two Spokesmen for Russia." *World Literatures.* Edited by Joseph Remenyi. Freeport, N.Y.: Books for Libraries Press, 1968.

Kartashev, A. V. *Ocherki po istoriy russkoy tserkvi.* [Essays on the history of the Russian church.] 2 vols. Paris: YMCA Press, 1959.

Kesich, Vesilin. "Some Religious Aspects of Dostoyevsky's 'Brothers Karamazov.'" *St. Vladimir's Seminary Quarterly* 9 (1965): 83–99.

Kohn, Hans. *Pan-Slavism: Its History and Ideology.* Notre Dame: University of Notre Dame Press, 1953.

———. *Prophets and People: Studies in Nineteenth Century Nationalism.* New York: Macmillan, 1946.

———., editor. *The Mind of Modern Russia.* New York: Harper and Row, 1962.

Kravchenko, Maria. *Dostoevsky and the Psychologists.* Amsterdam: Hakkert, 1978.

Lanckoronska, Karolina. *Studies on the Roman-Slavonic Rite in Poland.* Orientalia Christiana Analecta, no. 161. Rome: Pontificum Institutum Orientalium Studiorum, 1961.

Lewitter, L. R. "Peter the Great and the Polish Dissenters." *Slavonic and East European Review* 33 (1954): 75–101.

Lossky, Nikolay. *Dostoyevskiy i ego hristianskoe miroponimanie.* [Dostoevsky and his Christian worldview.] New York: Izdatel'stvo Imenni Chehova, 1953.

———. *History of Russian Philosophy.* New York: International Universities Press, 1951.

McKenzie, John L., S.J. *The Power and the Wisdom: An Interpretation of the New Testament.* Milwaukee: Bruce, 1965.

Mackiewicz, Stanislaw. *Dostoyevsky.* London: Orbis, 1948.

MacMaster, Robert. E. *Danilevsky: A Russian Totalitarian Philosopher.* Cambridge: Harvard University Press, 1967.

Magarshack, David. *Dostoevsky.* London: Secker and Warburg, 1962.

Makarii, Metropolitan of Moscow. *Istoriya russkoy tserkvi.* [The history of the Russian church.] 9 vols. Saint Petersburg: Tipographiya Kievo-Pecherskoy Yuliya Andr. Bokrama, 1866–79.

Malinin, Vasily N. *Starets eleazarova monastyria Filofey i ego poslaniya.* [Elder Filofey of the Eleazarov Monastery and his writings.] Kiev: Tipografiia Kievo-Pecherskoy Uspenskoy Lavry, 1901.

Manning, Clarence A. "Dostoyevsky and Scythism." *Sewanee Review* 33 (1925): 135–48.

Masaryk, Thomas G. *The Spirit of Russia.* 2 vols. New York: Macmillan, 1955.

Medlin, William K. *Moscow and East Rome: A Political Study of the Relations of Church and State in Muscovite Russia.* Geneva: Librairie E. Droz, 1952.

Merezhkovskiy, Dmitri S. *Tolstoy as Man and Artist: With an Essay on Dostoevsky.* New York: G. P. Putnam's Sons, 1902.

Miliukov, Paul. *Outlines of Russian Culture.* Philadelphia: University of Pennsylvania Press, 1948.

Mirsky, D. S. *A History of Russian Literature.* New York: Vintage, 1960.

Mochulsky, Konstantin. *Dostoevsky: His Life and Work.* Princeton: Princeton University Press, 1967.

Nørretranders, Bjarne. *The Shaping of Czardom Under Ivan Groznyj.* Copenhagen: Munksgaard, 1964.

Obolensky, Dmitri. "Byzantium, Kiev and Moscow: A Study in Ecclesiastical Relations." *Dumbarton Oaks Papers*, No. 11. Cambridge: Harvard University Press, 1957.

———. "Russia's Byzantine Heritage." *Oxford Slavonic Papers.* Vol. 1. Oxford: Clarendon Press, 1950.

O'Brien, Carl Bickford. *Muscovy and the Ukraine: From the Pereiaslavl Agreement to the Truce of Andrusovo, 1654–1667.* Berkeley: University of California Press, 1963.

Odoevsky, V. F. *Russian Nights*. New York: E. P. Dutton, 1965.

Olearius, Adam. *The Travels of Olearius in Seventeenth-Century Russia*. Translated and edited by Samuel S. Baron. Stanford: Stanford University Press, 1967

Palmer, William. *Notes of a Visit to the Russian Church*. Selected and arranged by Cardinal Newman. London: Longmans, Green and Co, 1895.

———. *The Patriarch and the Tsar*. 6 vols. London: Trubner and Co., 1871–76.

Pastor, Ludwig von. *The History of the Popes*. Vols. 35–40. Translated by E. F. Peeler. London: Routledge and Kegan Paul, 1952.

Paszkiewicz, Henryk. *The Making of the Russian Nation*. London: Darton, Longman and Todd, 1963.

———. *The Origin of Russia*. London: George Allen and Unwin, 1954.

Paul, Archdeacon of Aleppo. *The Travels of Macarius*. London: Oxford University Press, 1936.

Petrovich, Michael B. *The Emergence of Russian Pan-Slavism (1856–1870)*. New York: Columbia University Press, 1958..

Pierling, Paul, S.J. *Bathory et Possevino*. [Bathory and Possevino]. Paris: Ernest Lerous, 1887.

———. *Iz smutnago vremeni*. [From the time of troubles.] Saint Petersburg: A. S. Suvorin, 1902.

———. *Papes et Tsars: 1547–1597*. [Popes and tsars: 1547–1597]. Paris: Retaux-Bray, 1890.

———. *Rossiya i vostok*. [Russia and the East.] Saint Petersburg: S. Suvorin, 1892.

———. *La Russie et le Saint-Siège*. [Russia and the Holy See]. 5 vols. Paris: Plon-Nourrit, 1901–12.

Pipes, Richard, ed. *Karamzin's Memoir on Ancient and Modern Russia*. Cambridge: Harvard University Press, 1959.

Pollard, Albert F. *The Jesuits in Poland*. Oxford: B. H. Blackwell, 1892.

Pushkin, Alexander. *Boris Godunov*. Translated by Alfred Hayes. New York: E. P. Dutton, 1918.

Raeff, Marc, ed. *Russian Intellectual History: An Anthology*. New York: Harcourt, Brace and World, 1966.

Rahv, Philip. *The Myth and the Powerhouse.* New York: Farrar, Straus and Giroux, 1965.

Riasanovsky, Nicholas V. "Fourierism in Russia: An Estimate of the Petrassevcy." *American Slavic and East European Review* 12 (1953): 289–302.

———. *Russia and the West in the Teaching of the Slavophiles: A Study of Romantic Ideology.* Cambridge: Harvard University Press, 1952.

Rogger, Hans. *National Consciousness in Eighteenth Century Russia.* Cambridge: Harvard University Press, 1960.

———. "The Russian National Character: Some Eighteenth-Century Views." *Harvard Slavic Studies*, vol. 4. Cambridge: Harvard University Press, 1957.

Runciman, Steven. *The Eastern Schism: A Study of the Papacy and the Eastern Churches during the XIth and XIIth Centuries.* Oxford: Clarendon Press, 1955.

———. *The Fall of Constantinople 1453.* Cambridge: University Press, 1965.

———. *The Great Church in Captivity: A Study of the Patriarchate of Constantinople from the Eve of the Turkish Conquest to the Greek War of Independence.* Cambridge: University Press, 1968.

———. *A History of the Crusades.* 3 vols. Cambridge: Cambridge University Press, 1954.

Sandoz, Ellis. *The Grand Inquisitor: A Study in Political Apocalypse.* N. P., 1967.

Schreiber, Hermann. *Teuton and Slav: The Struggle for Central Europe.* New York: Alfred A. Knopf, 1965.

Segel, Harold B., ed. *The Literature of Eighteenth Century Russia.* New York: E. P. Dutton and Co., 1967.

Serech, Jury. "On Teofan Prokopovic as Writer and Preacher in His Kiev Period." *Harvard Slavic Studies*, vol. 7. Cambridge: Harvard University Press, 1954.

Seton-Watson, Hugh. *The Russian Empire 1801–1917.* Oxford: Clarendon Press, 1967.

Sevcenko, Ihor. "Intellectual Repercussions of the Council of Florence." *Church History* 24 (1955): 291–323.

Shestov, Lev. *Athens and Jerusalem.* Athens: Ohio University Press, 1966.

Simmons, E. J., ed. *Continuity and Change in Russian and Soviet Thought.* Cambridge: Harvard University Press, 1955.

Slonim, Marc. *Three Loves of Dostoevsky.* London: Alvin Redman, 1957.

Soloviev, Alexander V. *Holy Russia: The History of a Religious-Social idea.* The Hague: Mouton and Co., 1959.

Solovyov, Vladimir S. *Sobranie sochineniy.* [Complete works.] Saint Petersburg: Izdanie Tovarishchestva 'Obshchestvennaia Pol'za,' 1901.

Stender-Petersen, Adolf, and Stefan Congrat-Butlar, eds. *Anthology of Old Russian Literature.* New York: Columbia University Press, 1954.

Stremooukhoff, Dimitri. "Moscow the Third Rome: Sources of the Doctrine." *Speculum* 28 (1953): 84–101.

Tolstoy, Dmitry. *Le catholicisme romain en Russie.* [Roman Catholicism in Russia.] 2 vols. Paris: Dentu, Libraire-Editeur, 1863, 1864.

Toumanoff, Cyril. "Moscow the Third Rome; Genesis and Significance of a Politico-Religious Idea." *The Catholic Historical Review* 40 (1955): 411–47.

Turgenev, Ivan S. *Smoke.* New York: Dutton, 1949.

Vasiliev, A. A. "Was Old Russia a Vassal State of Byzantium?" *Speculum* 7 (1932): 350–60.

Vernadsky, George. *A History of Russia.* 5 vols. New Haven: Yale University Press, 1943–69.

——. "The Status of the Russian Church During the First Half-Century Following Vladimir's Conversion." *Slavonic and East European Review* 20 (1941): 294–314.

Voegelin, Eric, "The Mongol Orders of Submission to European Powers, 1245–1255." *Byzantion* 15 (1940–41): 378–413.

Waliszewski, K. *Ivan the Terrible.* Hamden, Conn.: Archon Books, 1966.

——. *Paul the First of Russia.* Hamden, Conn.: Archon Books, 1969.

——. *Peter the Great,* 2 vols. New York: Haskell House, 1969.

Walsh, Warren B. *Readings in Russian History.* 3 vols. Syracuse: Syracuse University Press, 1963.

Wasiolek, Edward, ed. *"The Brothers Karamazov" and the Critics.* Belmont, Calif.: Wadsworth Publishing Co., 1967.

——. *"Crime and Punishment" and the Critics.* San Francisco: Wadsworth Publishing Co., 1961.

Wellek, René, ed. *Dostoevsky: A Collection of Critical Essays.* Englewood Cliffs, N.J.: Prentice-Hall, Inc., 1962.

Winter, Eduard. *Russland und das Papsttum.* [Russia and the papacy] Berlin: Akademie-Verlag, 1961.

Wolff, Robert Lee. "The Three Romes: The Migration of an Ideology and the Making of an Autocrat." *Daedalus* 88 (1959): 291–311.

Yarmolinsky, Avrahm. *Dostoevsky: His Life and Art.* New York: Criterion Books, 1957.

——. *Dostoevsky: Works and Days.* New York: Funk and Wagnalls, 1971.

——. *Dostoievsky: A Study in His Ideology.* New York: N. P., 1921.

——. *Turgenev the Man, His Art and His Age.* New York: The Orion Press, 1959.

Zenkovsky, Serge A. *Medieval Russia's Epics, Chronicles, and Tales.* New York: E. P. Dutton, 1963.

——., ed. "The Russian Church Schism: Its Background and Repercussions." *The Russian Review* 16 (1957): 37–58.

Zenkovsky, Vasily V. *A History of Russian Philosophy.* 2 vols. London: Routledge and Kegan Paul, 1953.

——. *Russian Thinkers and Europe,* Ann Arbor: J. W. Edwards, 1953.

Zernov, Nicolas. *Three Russian Prophets: Khomiakov, Dostoevsky, Soloviev.* London: SCM Press, 1944.

——. "Vladimir and the Origin of the Russian Church." *The Slavonic Review* 28 (1949–50): 123–38; 425–38.

INDEX